SURVIVING STRONG-WILLED TODDLERS

BECOME A CALMER PARENT, COPE WITH TANTRUMS
AND RAISE YOUR TODDLER STRESS-FREE

SARAH HARGREAVES

CONTENTS

INTRODUCTION

In and out of itself, parenting is a full-time job. The effort it requires can be overwhelming, and when parents get exhausted, they may have various combinations of negative emotions such as guilt, despair, and sometimes even regret.

If parenting, in general, is that demanding, what about raising a strong-willed toddler? You need a defined map, one that has clear signs and instructions. That map is what you should use to guide you through raising a free-spirited toddler. That map is this guide. In this book, we will discuss the various areas of parenting that are necessary for your journey to survive strong-willed toddlers.

GROWTH AND DEVELOPMENT

B efore we get into detail regarding how to raise a strong-willed toddler in a positive environment, it is crucial that we first take a quick peek into the mind of toddlers, as explained by some of the experts on the subject. The purpose of this chapter is for you to learn and understand the growth processes taking place in the mind and life of your little one.

When talking about child development, names such as Skinner, Jean Piaget, and Erik Erikson come to mind. It is almost impossible to discuss child development stages without mentioning some of the stage theorists whose discoveries and theories still help guardians, teachers, parents, and caregivers even to this day. In this chapter, we will discuss some of these growth theories in relation to toddlers in order for you to draw a basic understanding of why your toddler acts and behaves the way they do. This is an important step toward spotting a strong-willed toddler.

Although definitions vary, toddlerhood runs from a child's first year to the time they turn three (CDC, 2020). Let us take a quick look into the developmental theories that help explain what is going on during your little one's toddlerhood, and then we will discuss exciting strategies that you can use to stay on top of your parenting game as your strong-willed toddler grows.

PIAGET'S THEORY OF COGNITIVE DEVELOPMENT

Each time one prematurely teaches a child something he could have discovered himself, that child is kept from inventing it and consequently from understanding it completely. –Jean Piaget

Jean Piaget was a Swiss psychologist whose work left a major mark on developmental psychology. Piaget had studied philosophy and zoology before he became fascinated by the thinking processes of school children, which led him to study the errors they make and the psychology of the mistakes. He later taught child psychology at university level, a profession he maintained up to his death, but still, his teachings live on (The Editors of Encyclopedia Britannica, 2018).

Piaget developed a concept that explains how strong-willed toddlers actively participate in the learning process through experience. He believed that although the quality of children's thinking is poorer than that of adults, children do not need someone to overwhelm them with knowledge and wisdom because they have to build on their experiences and learn from their mistakes. His theory of cognitive development has four stages, but in this book, we will only discuss the first two as they are the ones that best describe toddlerhood and early childhood.

Sensorimotor Stage

Piaget described the earliest phase of his cognitive development theory as a time of tremendous discoveries, changes, and growth. This stage occurs during your little one's first two years of life and is marked by their use of their innate senses such as smelling, hearing, touching, and seeing to learn more about the environment through trial and error. In addition to innate senses, your little one also uses acquired abilities such as grabbing, biting, and pushing. At this stage, your strong-willed toddler acquires experience and derives knowledge from it by using their senses and motor skills, hence the name of the phase. According to Piaget, your strong-willed toddler learns the difference between themselves and their surroundings, and they also begin to understand some important aspects, such as the concept of cause and effect. A strong-willed little one who understands the concept of causality is one who realizes that their physical actions have an effect on their environment. A simple example of this is when a toddler bites their mother while feeding, and the mother makes a face in response to the pain. Another example is when a toddler uses their hands or legs to push something, and the object resultantly moves.

This realization is an essential stepping stone toward your little one's later discovery of *object permanence*, the ability to understand that objects continue to exist even when they are out of sight. An experiment to test this skill in your little one during the early phase of their toddlerhood is by showing them something that catches their attention, then taking it out of their sight. If your strong-willed toddler has not yet developed object permanence, they will simply continue with their peaceful life, with the assumption that the item has ceased to exist. They will be at peace with their assumption and won't even try looking for the object. However, a strong-willed toddler who has acquired this skill is aware that the item is just out of sight but still exists. With that understanding, if the tiny human is interested in the hidden object, they will try looking for it.

Another achievement during the sensorimotor stage of cognitive development is *directed groping,* your little one's ability to pull and tilt items toward themselves for better access. The sensorimotor phase consists of six sub-stages, each marked by the acquisition of a new skill. Your strong-willed toddler has already passed some of these substages, but it is important for you to know what major skills they acquired at each subphase.

Reflexes

This substage is characterized by reflex actions and takes place during your little one's first month of birth. During this subphase, the tiny human responds to stimulation and studies the environment through inborn reflexes such as looking and sucking. A funny but true example of this is putting your nose close to their mouth. They will reflexively try to suck on it! At this point, they can suck on pretty much anything in or close to their mouth, be it a blanket or a bar of soap, and that is why parents and caregivers have to keep harmful items out of reach of their tiny ones.

Primary Circular Reactions

From their first to the fourth month of life, your bubbling bundle of joy goes through a developmental substage characterized by primary circular reactions. This subphase entails sensory coordination and the development of new schemas. Your little one will intentionally repeat actions that stimulate their body in a pleasurable way. Their actions during the primary circular reactions subphase are no longer reflexive but fully intended for the arousal they give. A common instance where this occurs is when they accidentally suck their thumb and find it enjoyable, so they repeat the sucking later, but this time on purpose. Another example is how they kick their legs while feeding.

Secondary Circular Reactions

After the primary circular reactions is another stage character-ized by secondary circular reactions. This one lasts from the time when your precious one is four months old until they reach eight months. During this subphase, their attention is drawn to the outside world, and they repeat pleasurable activities that involve not only their bodies but objects in their environment, as well. A relatable example is how your tiny human who is going through this subphase may shake a rattle while bathing just to enjoy the sound it produces. Another example is them picking up a toy to put it into their mouth if they find it fascinating.

Coordination of Reactions

During the fourth substage, from eight to twelve months, your little one begins to coordinate secondary reactions to create desired outcomes. Throughout this stage, they carry out clearly intentional activities instead of simply playing with their thumbs and toes. During this subphase, your bundle of joy actively explores their surroundings, frequently relating to the conduct of others. They also perceive some items as having distinct qualities, and they exhibit an ability to use their acquired knowledge to reach a goal. A demonstration of this achievement would be to have your little one look at something obstructing their toy from working. This could be a shoe or shirt blocking the movement of their toy car. Instead of just looking at it or finding something else to play with, if they have mastered coordination of reactions, they will reach out to try and remove the distraction.

Tertiary Circular Reactions

Between twelve to eighteen months is the fifth substage. It is characterized by tertiary circular reactions. The difference between this stage and the one it follows is that at this point, your strong-willed toddler displays intentional adaptations to particular situations. This is also the subphase during which they learn to experiment through trial and error. If your little one is hungry, for example, they may try different actions and experiment with various sounds to get your attention. They will remember whatever trick works and put it close to their heart for the next time they are in need of a similar result. They also try to fix the things *they* can, such as their toys, torn pages from books, or even broken pieces of glass. If they or someone drops a bottle, and it breaks, a strong-willed toddler who is developing well at this stage may voluntarily try putting the pieces together. Another example is if the toddler breaks their toy, they may try to bind the broken parts to restore functionality. They usually try to accomplish their fixing missions before their parent or caregiver notices any problem with the toys in order to avoid punishment.

Early Representational Thought

The final subphase of the sensorimotor stage starts at eighteen months and takes your strong-willed toddler all the way to their second birthday. Your little one now understands their environment through psychological processes rather than solely through actions at this period. They slowly gain the ability to form symbols in their mind to represent objects or events in the world. This is the point during which your little one develops the ability to mentally visualize objects that are not physically present, a crucial skill that they carry into the preoperational stage and continue to build on.

Preoperational Stage

After the sensorimotor stage of Piaget's theory of cognitive development comes the preoperational stage. This stage starts at the age of two and lasts until the age of seven. Although your strong-willed toddler can engage in symbolic play at this stage, they still lack the cognitive thinking to perform operations. Their thinking during this stage is therefore described as preoperational, meaning that it is before they acquire operational skills. This implies that they are unable to reason, change, mix, or separate thoughts. Despite being able to manipulate symbols, they do not understand concrete logic at the beginning of this phase. Their developmental changes are through adapting to new experiences in the world and moving toward the period during which they acquire concrete, logical reasoning.

Your little one builds on symbolic thought and employs symbols throughout the preoperational period. You can observe this in your strong-willed toddler by watching them play. They may intentionally use an item such as a shoe to symbolize something they are imagining, such as a house. Your little one may also have other people take part in their games and employ roleplaying. Because your precious one's imagination is clear, the playmates can be of any age range, and even pets can participate in the games. When roleplaying with their agemates, some may assume parenting roles while others remain the young ones. Depending on the games they want to play, this is the stage at which you can hear your strong-willed toddler trying to bark, purr, or even roar!

ERIKSON'S THEORY OF PSYCHOSOCIAL DEVELOPMENT

The attention and environment you provide shapes your child's brain development for life. –Erik Erikson

Another genius whose work left a mark on child development was a psychologist called Erik Erikson. He developed a theory that addressed the effects of social experience throughout one's entire lifespan. Erikson was interested in the role that social relations and interactions play in the development and growth of people.

With Erikson's theory of psychosocial development, each phase builds on the ones that came before it and prepares the way for the phases that follow it. He thought that we experience a conflict during each phase and that the conflict marks a turning point in development.

Erik Erikson's theory suggests that we either succeed or fail during each of the phases. If we succeed, we leave the stage with psychological strengths that will benefit us throughout our lives. We will experience a sense of mastery, also known as ego strength. If we fail, however, we do not acquire the crucial abilities required for a strong sense of self, and that lack haunts us for the rest of our lives. Erikson also believed that a sense of competence motivates behaviors and activities, so the focus of each of his stages is the development of this competence.

You must be wondering what Erikson's theories say about your little one, so let's get into it. His theory of psychosocial development has eight stages, from infancy to late adulthood, but in this book, we will only take a brief look into the first two because, well, we are talking about your strong-willed toddler.

Stage 1

The first stage of Erikson's theory describes the most fundamental period of your little one's life, the beginning. This stage runs from birth to around your little one's eighteenth month of life, and since toddlerhood occurs from the first to the third year, we will talk a little about the first stage.

Because a baby is entirely dependent, the dependability and caliber of their carers are the foundation for building trust. Your little one will learn whether to trust the adults around them based on the amount of attention they receive. If, for example, your little one gets hungry and cries but you ignore them, they will eventually learn that they cannot depend on you to give them food when they need it. If you provide your little one with their needs and shower them with love, they establish trust and will feel safe even as they grow. Your strong-willed little one gains a sense of trust when their caregivers are dependable, tender, and loving.

On the contrary, your precious one may develop mistrust if their caregivers are inconsistent, neglectful, or emotionally unavailable. Lack of trust will lead to fear and the idea that life is unpredictable and unstable.

Whether your little one succeeds or fails to achieve the goals of this developmental stage, their outcome will not be entirely positive or negative. Erikson believed that the key to effective development was achieving a balance between the two conflicting sides. What this means is that your little one will then develop hope and exercise a certain level of caution that danger can still exist, rather than completely trusting everyone they come across.

Stage 2

The second stage of Erikson's theory focuses on your strong-willed toddler gaining more self-control. At this point, they gain a little independence. Your toddler learns to carry out some tasks on their own, and they even develop their own preferences. You can support their feeling of autonomy by giving them the freedom to choose and take charge.

This is the time for the potty, but remember that the main point of this stage is for your strong-willed toddler to gain independence and personal control over their physical abilities. You can help them by exercising patience when they try to do something by themself, instead of rushing them through the process or doing it yourself.

Toilet training is a common example to demonstrate this process. Other examples involve your little one gaining more control over their food preferences, the toys they like, and even the clothes they want to wear. If your strong-willed toddler is having challenges with the developmental milestones of this stage, or if you do not support their preferences, they may lose their sense of freedom. Failure to achieve the goals at this stage arouses feelings of shame and uncertainty in them, whereas success establishes autonomy.

INTERACTIVE ACTIVITIES

Your bubbling toddler loves playtime, but figuring out suitable activities for such a tiny human being can be difficult. You may worry about the possibility of them getting hurt or overwhelming them with tasks that extend beyond their current abilities. Strong-willed toddlers are special, and you may realize that even after spending days choosing suitable activities for them, they may not like your taste. Just as bluntly as that, they may get bored and decide to do something else. You may throw your hands in the air and give up in disappointment, but you don't want to miss out on real fun, do you?

There are plenty of activities you can do with your little one. When picking activities for a strong-willed toddler, you would do well to pick ones that will give them a challenge because these kids love a good challenge. I'm not saying you should play chess and sudoku with them just because they are spirited, but you have a variety of choices. You don't need to keep a thousand activities, just the ones you can, and then you simply repeat those until they outgrow them. Even then, you can modify them a little to make them more challenging and suit your toddler's development stage.

Before you choose, you want to make sure that your pick is right. You want to consider what makes *one* activity better than the rest. Below are a few things to consider as you evaluate your options for the best fit.

• your toddler's abilities

Whether or not a certain activity is the right choice for your strong-willed toddler depends on their range of abilities and the developmental milestones they are working on.

• the learning outcomes of the activity

As much as you want the activities to be a fun way to entertain your toddler while improving your bonding time, they also have to present developmental benefits that favor your strong-willed toddler's growth.

• how much time the activity takes

You have to put your schedule into consideration when picking interactive activities for your toddler because you don't want to be stuck at home all day. Your strong-willed toddler may also get bored of doing the same activity over and over.

• your toddler's interests

Playing with your strong-willed toddler can become challenging if you dictate the activities, so you have to involve them in the decision-making. Remember, they have challenges with being told what to do, so you avoid conflict by letting them exercise control.

If you take all these important factors into consideration when picking the most suitable activity for your strong-willed toddler, you reduce chances of your little one losing interest or refusing to take part in the activities.

PLAY-BASED LEARNING

You have likely heard the expression that children are like sponges, and while that is generally true, it is especially true for toddlers. Playing is the primary means by which they acquire knowledge. You can improve your spirited toddler's emotional, cognitive, and physical capabilities with the right kind of play. You can introduce your strong-willed toddler to productive play time by teaching them some easy games that are both fun and educational. Your little one will begin by playing alongside their mates, a tactic called side-by-side play. From there, they then progress to more interactive activities, during which they mingle with their playmates and gain information.

Games

Your strong-willed toddler's intellectual, physical, and emotional abilities significantly improve when you implement play-based learning to help them discover useful tactics for their development as well as develop beneficial skills to aid their growth. At the same time, they still get to do something they can enjoy. Introducing your strong-willed toddler to educational games will also help mend some unfavorable behaviors, such as preferring to play alone, while encouraging positive ones such as developing empathy. You can get your tiny human started with some of the games below.

Simon Says

A time-honored activity that instills in young minds the importance of attentively following directions, Simon Says is a game that your strong-willed toddler can play alone or with friends. The rules are straightforward: When you take on the role of Simon, what you say is taken seriously. Your strong-willed toddler then has to comply with the commands that you give them. You could tell them that Simon says that they should count to five, and they will count because, well, Simon says so. They must keep their ears peeled for the words *Simon says...* If they shout out commands without first telling Simon, players risk elimination from the game. Be sure to include some amusing orders to keep your strong-willed toddler interested. You can instruct them to wink, jump like a frog, wiggle their hands the way their dog wiggles its tail, and many other funny commands.

I'll Give You Mine, and You Give Me Yours

This is an excellent game for strong-willed toddlers because it encourages cooperation. Put together a collection of items such as crayons, puzzle pieces, or buttons, and then have your strong-willed toddler give you one of the items and get one for themselves. Make sure each of you has a container to hold your collections of items. This game teaches your spirited toddler to share their belongings with those around them.

Hokey-Pokey

Another time-honored game, this one is not only incredibly entertaining but will also teach your strong-willed toddler how to follow directions and identify the various parts of their body. The song *Hokey-Pokey* is a straightforward tune with lyrics that provide instructions. Playing is simple. All your strong-willed toddler has to do is follow instructions from the song's lyrics.

Parachute

This game is fun when there are more than two people participating. Place a light bedsheet, big plastic, or (if you have access to one) a parachute on the ground. Have everyone grab one of the edges with both hands and hold it firmly. You can slowly raise it above your head while shouting "Up, up, up!" then lower it while shouting "Down, down, down!" The moment you shout "Down, down, down," everyone has to release their grip on the sheet and make their way underneath it. This game teaches your free-spirited toddler to learn to wait their turn and listen more attentively. It also helps them develop their motor skills as they grow.

Treasure Hunt

Is there anything more exciting than going on a hunt for buried treasure? Give your strong-willed toddler specific instructions on what to look for and have them search the house for the items. For instance, you can ask your toddler to find a red shoe in the house if you want to improve their knowledge of colors. Alternatively, you can have them bring you two empty cups from the kitchen to test their ability to count. If your strong-willed toddler is able to do those things, then congratulations; you can move to a more complex stage where you can have your toddler bring you two blue jackets. That way, you test their color recognition skills and their ability to count. You can also ask them to randomly choose an item and then question them about the object's characteristics.

Hide-and-Seek

If you remember the developmental theories we covered at the beginning of this book, you may remember that your strong-willed toddler is at a stage during which they are building on object permanence. Hiding from them and having them find you is a great way to teach them problem-solving. If you would rather not hide, you can always ask your strong-willed toddler to hide somewhere in the house then you set off to find them.

Obstacle Course

This game is all about having fun while improving your strong-willed toddler's balance, coordination, and gross motor skills. They can roll, jump, and run over or under objects or markers if you set up a small track for them in your living room or outside in the yard, depending on how much space you have available.

Puzzles

Putting puzzle pieces together requires your strong-willed toddler to exercise their motor, cognitive, and emotional skills. For that reason, puzzles make excellent games for your spirited toddler who has to learn to be more patient. Constructing a puzzle can also serve to exercise your strong-willed toddler's memory, teach them various shapes, and assist them in setting straightforward objectives.

Odd One Out

In front of your little one, arrange several blocks of the same color, and ensure you include at least one block of a different color in the arrangement. Have them look at the set blocks, then ask them to identify the block that is different from the others. You can increase the difficulty of this game by using flashcards of different shapes or plants and then asking your strong-willed toddler to identify which ones are the same and which are different.

Musical Chairs

Playing musical chairs teaches strong-willed toddlers to settle disagreements without resorting to violence, cope with disappointment, and hone their patience. Arrange chairs in a circle, omitting one chair such that the number of players exceeds the number of available chairs. Play music while the toddlers walk around the circle of chairs. When the music stops, the players should attempt to find a chair to sit on. The toddlers who are unable to secure a seat will be excluded from the next round of the game. After that, take out one more chair, and start over.

Strong-willed toddlers have to learn to deal with the frustration of being left out, which requires them to practice patience and wait graciously. In addition to this, they need to learn how to use their words to resolve disagreements regarding whose chair is whose or who got it first. Be sure to have an adult present specifically to ensure that the toddlers resolve disagreements amicably, as well as to provide moral support for those who are no longer participating in the game. That will teach your little ones to have a positive outlook on situations and to understand that if they want second chances, they have to be willing to put in the necessary amount of work. In this case, waiting is the price of a second chance.

There are several other educational games that you can introduce to your strong-willed toddler to encourage proper development. You can also alter some elements of the games to emphasize the qualities you feel your strong-willed toddler needs to work more on.

2

SPOTTING A STRONG-WILLED TODDLER

W hat exactly does it mean for a toddler to be strong-willed? Some parents describe their little ones as stressful or stubborn, while others, more positively, describe them as free-spirited. However, there is another way to look at strong-willed toddlers: as little humans of integrity who are not easily swayed from their own point of view. Strong-willed toddlers tend to be courageous, enduring, and full of life. They prefer to discover things for themselves instead of blindly acknowledging what others have to say about them, which is why they continue to push the boundaries around them and their situations. They have a strong desire to be responsible for themselves and, at times, put their need to be right ahead of everything else on their list of priorities. When their attention is fully focused on one thing, their brain appears to have difficulty shifting gears. Strong-willed or free-spirited toddlers have intense feelings of passion and move through life at breakneck speed.

Imagine you are eating a nutritious meal that has a lot of veggies, you offer the same meal to your spirited toddler, but they spit it out to stage a mini protest. The more you try to get them to eat it, the more they might resist or even start crying that they want something meaty or sweet because, well, whose toddler doesn't love candy? As time passes and your little one's behavior persists, you gradually start noticing that your strong-willed toddler just wants to do what they want. You realize that they simply want things their own way. At that moment, you can assure yourself that you are not just raising a tiny human; you are facing a strong-willed toddler, one who is not afraid to stand up for their ideas, decisions, and emotions, one who dares to prevail!

Strong-willed toddlers find it intolerable when their parents tell them what to do, which, to some extent, is true even for several adults. However, when a toddler displays that kind of behavior, it is a whole new level of seeing the world. Even when setting boundaries, parents and caregivers who have strong-willed toddlers should make an effort to ensure their toddlers feel understood. That simple hack will help prevent power struggles from occurring in the future. As a parent or caregiver, make an effort to empathize with others, think critically, and recognize that mutual respect is a two-way street. The pursuit of solutions that are beneficial to all parties involved rather than the simple establishment of the law helps prevent strong-willed toddlers from growing into dangerous explosives and teaches them essential negotiation skills as well as the ability to compromise.

Toddlers who have a strong will are more than just resilient. If someone coerces them into submitting to the will of others, they believe that their integrity has been compromised. They are willing to cooperate without complaint so long as they retain the right to vote. If this bothers you due to the fact that you believe obedience is important quality, I would ask you to rethink that belief. You should always strive to bring up a strong-willed toddler who is responsible, caring, and cooperative, who will choose to do the right thing even when circumstances are difficult and swerving toward the wrong side seems inevitable. However, this does not imply that you should force or try to rewire their brain to obey you; it means you should encourage them to act in a morally upright manner because it is what *they* believe and want for themself.

The perception that one has of a toddler's strong will often determine whether that toddler is seen in an extremely positive or extremely negative light. Is it, therefore, detrimental for your little one to have a strong will? In no way should you believe that to be the case. Being a strong-willed toddler certainly has its advantages, and if you raise your little one right, their strong-will will be their ticket to a happy and successful life in the future. Strong-willed toddlers grow up to be determined and resolute. When parents and caregivers nurture their strong-willed toddlers with love and care, encouraging the best out of their little ones, the determination and resolution that strong-willed toddlers exhibit are extremely desirable characteristics. If they grow up in a positive environment and receive the right kind of guidance, strong-willed toddlers have the potential to grow into excellent leaders. On the other hand, if they do not receive enough warmth and miss out on positive parenting, strong-willed toddlers may come across as rigid and irritable. With time, the effects of growing up in a negative parenting environment kick in, shaping negative characteristics into undesirable behaviors such as aggression.

PERSONALITY AND TEMPERAMENT

When we consider temperament and personality, we see that the two are related to one another and that they both emerge at a young age. These are two characteristics that must be fostered from an early age because they stay with us throughout our lives.

What exactly does it mean for your toddler to have a temperament? It is a term that refers to the various facets of your little one's personality, such as their level of extroversion or introversion. Temperament is not something that you can teach your toddler to have; rather, it is a set of natural qualities that they are born with. On the other hand, their personality refers to a set of qualities that develop within your toddler over time. Certain patterns, such as those involving behavior, feelings, and thoughts, make up your little one's personality, which is something that persists throughout their lifetime. Consistency, the ability to have a psychological and physiological impact on behaviors and actions, as well as your toddler's ability to express themself in a variety of ways, are all fundamental aspects of their personality.

Temperament is an innate mannerism that can be passed down through generations, while personality develops in response to your toddler's temperament. It is also possible to say that your little one's temperament is their emotional activity. Studying and understanding your little one's temperament is always one of the best things you can do as a parent or caregiver because it assists you in better appreciating your toddler's capabilities and limitations. While it is true that your toddler's temperament is innate to them, they also build on it and continue to develop it over time. In the same way that a person's personality evolves over time, the way you carry yourself and treat your little one has a significant influence on how your strong-willed toddler further develops their temperament.

Personality is something that your little one will develop over the course of their adventurous life. It can be influenced by a variety of factors, including education, socialization, the various pressures they may face in life, and other factors as well. If you are familiar with your little one's temperament, you will be able to anticipate whether they will approach the upcoming developmental milestones with enthusiasm, proceed with caution, or hesitantly turn away.

Temperament

How would you describe your little one's temperament? In general, your toddler's demeanor can be classified as laid-back, timid, or fiery. Below are brief explanations of the three basic categories.

Easygoing Temperament

Roughly half of the toddlers who are easygoing do not seem bothered by anything. They feel optimistic and prepared to face the new day when they wake up feeling good. They are outgoing (but not reckless), adaptable, and enthusiastic about meeting new people and experiencing new things. Easygoing toddlers are also resilient and can quickly bounce back from setbacks and disappointments with a smile on their faces.

Slow to Warm Temperament

Some toddlers are reserved, wary, and slow to open up to novel experiences. By the age of about nine months, most outgoing babies will smile at passing strangers, while reserved babies, on the other hand, will frown and cling to their parents or caregivers for safety and reassurance. If you have visitors at home, a shy toddler may often stay glued to their seat and will be comfortable —if not relieved—watching the guests leave without saying goodbye or even spraying them a smile. Toddlers who are cautious are frequently more sensitive than their peers. They don't like their food to be too cold and don't like it when their pants are itchy. They are prone to frustration, anxiousness, and clinginess and do not adapt well to change. Reserved toddlers are cautious and almost always turn out to be keen observers because they spend more time watching than they do actively getting involved. These are the kinds of toddlers who, upon realizing where they are going, might start crying even before they reach the pediatrician's office if they do not feel comfortable there. They are frequently among the first to speak but among the last to leave, and they often avoid doing things if they are in doubt or if anything feels wrong.

Reserved toddlers may alternate between dependence on their parents or caregivers and their yearning for independence. This can be a little difficult to handle, but if you treat them with patience and respect, they will graduate from their toddlerhood happy and full of self-assurance. It is important that little ones who are reserved and cautious be shielded from excessive pressure and criticism. When exposed to rejection and harsh judgment, timid toddlers may spend the rest of their life feeling anxious and rigid.

Difficult Temperament

Strong-willed toddlers are not very common. These headstrong toddlers experience both highs and lows throughout their lives. When the sparks of everyday stress combine with part of their personality, the result tends to be disastrous. The majority of the time, parents and caregivers are able to recognize whether or not they have a strong-willed little one because these toddlers have more prominent traits than other toddlers. They are more active, impatient, impulsive, rebellious, rigid, intense, and sensitive.

Determining Temperament

You can learn about the characteristics that are associated with each temperament type to determine what ways your toddler best embodies the characteristics.

Some of the characteristics of a calm and easygoing toddler include:

- cheerful demeanor
- not easily affected by noise or strong odors
- swift to adapt to change
- consistent eating patterns
- understanding that things may not always go their way
- genuine interest in making new acquaintances

Some of the characteristics of a slow to warm temperament in your toddler include:

- preference for peaceful play
- focused and selectively sensitive to sounds and odors
- slight discomfort when interacting with new individuals
- joyfulness
- regular eating and sleep patterns that are easy to predict
- challenges dealing with unforeseen changes
- intimidation by unexpected events
- gentle to passionate feelings

Some of the characteristics of difficult or free-spirited temperament in your toddler:

- restlessness
- relentlessness
- insensitive to smells and sounds
- easily distracted
- highly active
- irregular sleep patterns
- unpredictable eating habits

Personality

Everyone eventually develops their own distinct personality and set of characteristics. If you are aware of your toddler's temperament, you will be better able to comprehend the reasons behind their actions and reactions. Additionally, knowing their personality assists you in resolving any behavioral issues they may exhibit. Hippocrates came up with four primary classifications to explain an individual's personality. There is a possibility that your mini human possesses qualities that are associated with more than one group, so there are times when a loose classification is more appropriate than trying to bundle everything under one personality classification. It is not uncommon for your toddler to exhibit the characteristics of a single personality type more prominently than those of other personality classes. Below are the four personality classes as identified by Hippocrates.

Sanguine

If your toddler has a sanguine personality, they are the talkative, inventive, and playful type. They also enjoy playing games. Toddlers with sanguine personality traits are often easygoing, optimistic, and daring and do not shy away from taking risks. These toddlers are at risk of developing boredom and having difficulty if their environment fails to provide them with enough amusement.

Choleric

Passionate, talkative, competitive, determined, strong-willed, and adventurous best describe tiny humans with a choleric personality. Choleric toddlers are typically goal-oriented and have the ability to express commendable rationality and analytical thinking.

Phlegmatic

This character trait is characterized by thoughtfulness, control, diplomacy, and a controlled demeanor. Toddlers who have phlegmatic personality types tend to require deep personal interactions. They are devoted and take pleasure in assisting others. Phlegmatic toddlers also try their best to steer clear of confrontation.

Melancholic

Observant toddlers who are detailed, polite, orderly, and attentive possess traits of the melancholic personality class. Melancholic toddlers are very outgoing and eager to assist others in any way they can. These mini-humans do not have the same passion for excitement and peril as those who have qualities of other personality classes.

Extroversion and Introversion

This aspect of your little one's development pertains to their attention being more versed on either the inside or the outside. Extroverted toddlers tend to be gregarious and talkative, whereas those who are introverted tend to be quieter and more reflective. Extroverted toddlers use more of their energy on their external environment than introverted toddlers who focus more on their inner self than the outside world.

Characteristics of Strong-Willed Toddlers

Some toddlers continually display specific characteristics, despite the fact that all toddlers are capable of developing strong will at some point or another. The temperaments of strong-willed toddlers often become apparent at an extremely early phase of their life. Being a good toddler and being strong-willed are two entirely different things. Strong-willed toddlers simply want to accomplish things on their own terms when they participate in home, school, or social settings. Their stubbornness can make their interaction with friends and adults quite difficult. It might be challenging to get a toddler who has a strong sense of independence to do something that they do not want to do. If your little one displays many of these characteristics, the most important thing you can do is not try to squash their spirit but rather discover ways to assist them in channeling their energy into something constructive.

Furious Rage

Even though every tiny human can have temper tantrums, strong-willed toddlers display extreme rage that can last for extended periods. They have a low frustration threshold and have difficulty expressing their anger in a manner that most would consider to be socially acceptable. It gets worse because there are situations when you might not even be sure what triggered them in the first place.

Entitlement

Several toddlers who feel entitled have trouble telling the difference between what they *need* to do and what they *want* to do. Strong-willed toddlers also place a significant emphasis on fairness. They may insist, even when everything is going just fine, that they are not getting their fair portion of food or that they have not had enough time to play with their toys because you had given them tasks to carry out.

Stubbornness

They only hear, feel, or see what they want. Strong-willed toddlers can simply ignore you if they are not interested in what you have to say. Such toddlers who are willing to participate in their own activities are adept at using selective hearing, and they have a tendency to overlook anything that does not fulfill their requirements.

Need for Justification

Many spirited toddlers find it upsetting when you tell them to do something without providing them with a reason. They are curious as to why they are not allowed to play in the rain and why you always say that dancing on the sofa is unacceptable. Your spirited toddler will not be content with answers that show uncertainty or feel dismissive. If you want your strong-willed toddler to quit fighting, they will expect you to explain why this is a problem as well as what you are basing that reason on.

Persistence

When they disagree with something, spirited toddlers do not give up. They take pleasure in engaging in power confrontations, and the people around them often become exhausted as a result of that intransigence. They are excellent communicators who are also skilled at locating gaps in reasoning and making exceptions. Therefore, you should not be surprised if your strong-willed toddler recalls that you once forced them to have ice cream for breakfast or any other *harmless* lie you may have cooked up in the past as a way to escape a situation you did not want to stay in.

Arrogance

Toddlers who have a strong sense of will tend to have a clear mental picture of how they think things should be and often plot out ways to make that image a reality. They have no issue directing their friends on where to go or how to act, and they also have no problem giving adults advice about what they should and should not be doing.

Personal Guidelines

Toddlers who have a strong sense of independence almost do not care what you think. For example, when it is time for them to go to bed, they can be adamant about going to bed *when* they feel sleepy. A strong-willed toddler is more interested in formulating their own policies and establishing their own standards than they are in adhering to the regulations established by an authority figure, especially if the authority figure did not invest time in helping the toddler understand the logic behind those rules. Spirited toddlers also do things when they have the desire to do so. They may eat or talk quickly when it suits their mood, and they may complete their tasks pretty fast if their minds tell them that they have something even more important to get to. When they are engaged in an activity that does not pique their attention, however, they feel free to move at a snail's pace.

Decisiveness

You are wasting your time and energy if you try to persuade a strong-willed toddler to do something they do not want to do. You will not get very far by harassing, pleading, or trying to rationalize what you want over what they want. A strong-willed toddler is difficult to convince and will dig in their heels, refusing to budge because they almost always have their mind made up.

Impatience

Several strong-willed toddlers want to plan everything according to their own agenda. They despise having to wait their turn when playing a game, they are against sitting in the waiting room at the doctor's office, and they despise having to stand in line when you go to the grocery store with them. Spirited toddlers are often against squandering even a single second waiting for something or someone.

3

ACCEPTING YOUR TODDLER

V arious people across the world have different views regarding strong-willed toddlers. The difference in views contributes to misunderstandings about what a strong-willed toddler really is. Some people will tell you that a strong-willed toddler is one who is rude and disrespectful, while others will tell you that a strong-willed toddler is immensely difficult. However, the simplest, clearest explanation you can find as to what a strong-willed toddler is lies in the word itself: they have a strong will. That is all, and that is enough. It is essential for you to have an understanding of these widely held misconceptions in order to effectively advocate for your strong-willed toddler, who will most often be misunderstood by many. We need to put an end to the stigma and get rid of these outdated schools of thought if we want to be successful in the task of bringing up our proud toddlers, that is, teaching them right from wrong without compromising their bravery.

WHAT A STRONG-WILLED TODDLER IS NOT

Let us bust the myths of what has been said about free-spirited toddlers.

- Strong-willed toddlers automatically have thick skin.

Free-spirited toddlers earn the reputation of being resilient. In fact, most of the time, they are highly sensitive beings. They have a sensitive heart and equally exaggerated emotional responses, and they are highly attuned to changes in their surrounding environment. For example, if there is a heated argument among toddlers about who plays with a red toy car, despite presenting as a dominant figure, if your strong-willed toddler does not get the toy, they might cry about it and express their emotions when you have a one-on-one talk. They may even confess to you how bad they feel for trying to be selfish and only assuming they are the only one who wants to play with the toy.

Strong-willed toddlers can give the impression that they are tough when they insist that things be done in a particular way. However, their sharp exterior often serves to mask sensitivity and personal conflict within their inner self.

- Strong-willed toddlers are obstinate.

The personality traits that are present in an infant at birth are referred to as their temperament in the field of developmental psychology. Strong-willed toddlers are often described as difficult and recalcitrant due to their strong standing temperament. Your strong-willed toddler will not behave the same way as other toddlers because the wiring in their brains is different. It will be easier for you to connect with your little ones if you master the art of exerting authority over them without resorting to violence or dictatorship.

- Strong-willed toddlers will try to exert their authority over you.

Several people have the misconception that strong-willed toddlers want to be in charge of the people around them. Although strong-willed toddlers have a better chance of succeeding as leaders, their need for control is not aimed at the people around them, but at the situations they find themselves in as well as those to come. Your strong-willed toddler won't try to exert their authority on you, but they will strive to exert dominance over certain circumstances—that is the distinction. They place a high value on consistency and are willing to dedicate significant effort in order to feel secure and safe.

- Strong-willed toddlers are uncontrollable.

Some individuals typically portray strong-willed toddlers as wildly self-assured little ones. Despite their admirable qualities, strong-willed toddlers have a high sensitivity level and a profound level of thought. These qualities can make it difficult for parents and caregivers to rule over these little humans. Some strong-willed toddlers may suffer from other health conditions that affect the way they act and react, such as attention deficit hyperactivity disorder (ADHD). If your strong-willed toddler is uncontrollable, you may realize that those control issues stem from conditions deeper than their temperament, such as anxiety.

WHAT A STRONG-WILLED TODDLER IS

- They are your opportunity to learn and your chance to improve.

Your strong-willed toddler will improve the way you care for yourself. They can be full of energy and challenging in a positive way. If you decide to go out in the park with your little one, they will be running around at a faster pace than you, which will help you reignite your lost energy, challenging you to stay fit. Your curious little one will ask a lot of questions, some of which you won't even have answers to. That will challenge you to learn more about the subjects your toddler finds fascinating so that the next time they ask, you provide them with the right answers.

- They facilitate your self-discovery.

If your strong-willed toddler continuously displays certain unacceptable behaviors such as anger outbursts, violence, or cursing, you might find it a difficult situation to cope with and decide to go for therapy. Your therapist will focus on you, how you were brought up, your usual behavior at home, and many other facets that could be contributing to your toddler's behavior through your parenting approaches. Your therapist may ask if you have any anger issues, if you are depressed, or if you are going through other tough times. If you have any mental health difficulties, you might be surprised to learn that your behavior can be passed down and reflected in the way your strong-willed toddler acts and reacts. It is incredible how much you can discover about yourself if you look at things in an objective manner.

• They encourage your pursuit of balance.

When you have a little one who is always active, your parenting days won't be all candy and roses. Your toddler will want to have an uninterrupted day of high-speed fun right up until the point where it all goes up in flames. To meet their robust amount of energy, you must first achieve balance in your life. You can revisit the things you used to do before parenting overtook your life. The things that once made you happy and kept you sane. These can be any simple activities that help you relieve stress, such as taking part in your favorite sport or meditating. When you attain a state of equilibrium within yourself, you become recalibrated and re-energized, and you become well-equipped to live another busy day with your energetic toddler.

• They have the potential to improve your willpower.

The makeup of our society is constantly shifting. We are inun-dated with information about almost everything, some of which are correct and other bits that are false. The world we live in is fraught with intense competition and can be challenging to navi-gate at times. The qualities of your toddler's temperament will serve them well even when they grow up because they are not afraid to try new things and enjoy what they do to the fullest regardless of the consequences or external judgment. This can encourage you to do better and not give up even if people and the universe seem convinced about your impending failure.

Positive Qualities of a Strong-Willed Toddler

It is much easier to see your wayward toddler for who they truly are when you try and view their actions and reactions from an objective viewpoint. Your little human being is in the process of learning how to interact with the outside world, and their inborn temperament facilitates that development. Your cute little human should not have to exist as an object of your control or desires but rather as a one-of-a-kind individual who already possesses strong characteristics that are necessary for them to endure and prosper in the world. There is no question that parenting a strong-willed toddler is more challenging than raising the usual toddler. Because of your free-spirited toddler, you are constantly being challenged to develop new skills in the areas of communication and leadership. You will find yourself faced with the need to make a lot of difficult decisions and sacrifices beyond your comfort zone, but in the end, your strong-willed toddler is worth all that. With that said, let us take a look at the advantages of having a strong-willed toddler.

Determination

If you ask your strong-willed toddler to stop playing with their building blocks, but they just throw a brief glance in your direction and then refocus on their blocks, it might appear as though they did not hear you. What really happens is that their mind is set on constructing whatever they are building, and until that boat or house stands tall, their job is unfinished. If their job is unfinished, they have nowhere else to be but at work! That is the kind of toddler you have—a determined, busy body. Many strong-willed toddlers have a tendency to get stuck in their own cognitive trajectory of what they think is important and may have difficulties developing the mental flexibility required to make necessary cognitive shifts. Your toddler's level of determination will contribute to how hard they work to achieve both small and large life goals, such as using their building blocks to construct a house or later using available resources to attain a master's degree.

Passion

If your three-year-old toddler fixes their mind on constructing a log cabin in the living room, you will be amazed at how well they are able to concentrate and engage in the activity. It will seem to you as though your little one is in their own tiny world, and indeed, they would be. Your strong-willed toddler is a creative thinker who dares to send their mind outside the box and uncover new findings. They are willing to participate in new endeavors and ideas with a great deal of passion and enthusiasm. Passion is your little one's guiding star. It walks them through determining where and how they want to share their ideas and talents with those around them. Your strong-willed toddler's passion makes them more involved, committed, and satisfied with the activities they enjoy as well as the energy and effort they put in.

Conviction

If you treat your strong-willed toddler with disrespect or betray their trust, they will develop a strong sense of conviction. For example, if you tell your little one you will give them candy if they eat up the veggies on their plate, then you keep dodging and postponing when it is time to fulfill your end of the bargain, they will take you for a liar because that makes them realize they cannot rely on you to keep your word. Because your little one was born with a robust sense of integrity and morality, it will be difficult for them to take the context of the situation into account when it comes to their perception of right and wrong. They will take a firm stance and defend their beliefs.

Guidance

Your strong-willed toddler is not one to hesitate to seize control and guide the rest of their friends. When playing at the playground, your little one may often take the lead in organizing what games to play as well as deciding who goes and who stays. As they grow, your toddler may even reach a point at which they can guide their playmates when it is time to go home or play a different game. Due to their strong resolve, it is easy for your little one to take on responsibilities and lead others. Because of the fact that following orders is not one of their strong points, it can be challenging for your strong-willed toddler to take the guidance of others. Although they will need additional support from friends and other adults to remember important social skills such as communication and collaboration, your strong-willed toddler will have a natural and clear understanding of the big picture. They will also have a good chance of becoming successful leaders in the future.

Perseverance

If your headstrong toddler has expressed interest in getting a pet, they will not stop talking about that cat, dog, or rabbit until they finally get one. This relentlessness stems from an inner quest that is as inherent to your strong-willed toddler as blinking is. This perseverance means great things await your strong-willed toddler, and all you have to do is shower them with support and motivate them to aim higher. Whenever you think your little one's relentlessness is becoming a little too much, remind yourself that they will be able to overcome major challenges in the future because of their enduring nature. This quality is your strong-willed toddler's inner strength and will help them stand strong when others their age waver and give up.

Cooperation

Your little one has a strong sense of personal integrity, which causes them to become agitated whenever you resort to physical force or exert obvious control as a method of communicating. If you continuously try to make your strong-willed toddler do things because you are the adult, you may continue to face resistance until you modify your communication tactics. You may find it beneficial to improve communication by learning to speak in a tone that encourages cooperation and positivity even when disciplining your strong-willed toddler.

Enthusiasm

You may find that your little one moves and talks more than your friends' toddlers, and you may worry that your strong-willed toddler will annoy your elderly relatives, who probably still believe that toddlers should be seen and not heard. It can be exhausting to try to keep your smart and active toddler occupied on a slow Saturday, but if you encourage them to channel that contagious energy and enthusiasm into public speaking or an energetic career such as education, it will be a force for positivity and fun.

4

PARENTS AND FEELINGS

R aising a toddler is no easy battle, don't let anyone convince
you otherwise. That is far from your case, though—yours is
a special one. You are parenting a strong-willed toddler, and that is
what sets your parenting journey apart from what most parents
and caregivers have to deal with. While your fellow parents and
caregivers are dealing with late-night feeding, you have to stand
strong amidst unwarranted tantrums and unjustified meltdowns.
You are the parent or caregiver who has to stand up and defend
their position lest their tiny human claims it first!

PARENTING BURNOUT

Are you feeling overwhelmed by the responsibilities that come
with parenting a strong-willed toddler, such as assisting with their
homework even when they want to stick to their own mini schedule, encouraging them to clean up after they eat, or maybe
throwing them parties to encourage social interaction? When you
first got this parenting job of yours and made a lifetime commit-
ment, did you accept the fact that feeling overwhelmed was going

to be a part of the job? Even if you did expect that the road would be rocky and the job overwhelming, you might not have realized the level of difficulty it entailed until you got there, and now here you are. If you feel like you have reached your limit of endurance and are unsure what to do next, then you might be close to burning out.

Raising a strong-willed toddler can result in mental, emotional, and physical exhaustion that leaves you drowning in a pool of disturbing emotions. That state is called parenting burnout and can leave you sad, depressed, and overwhelmed. Try looking at things from a different angle, tackling your parenting challenges one at a time. Beware of how much influence you give these challenges over your life because if you let them, they can eat you up before you even solve your parenting challenges. Conduct an analysis to determine the extent to which you are contributing to the various challenges you are encountering. Seek assistance from other people and keep your mind open to therapy.

Signs You are Burning Out

Each parent or caregiver has their own way of handling emotions and situations, and that is why burnout impacts each individual differently. The effect of parenting burnout is case-dependent, but here are some of the most common symptoms of parenting burnout when raising a strong-willed toddler:

- despair
- self-doubt
- exhaustion
- recurrent headaches
- irritability
- body pains
- appetite fluctuations

- feeling alone
- substance abuse
- poor sleeping habits
- weight loss
- demotivation

The good thing about this is that you don't just wake up burnt out one day. It is a process that builds up as a result of various unaddressed feelings throughout your parenting journey. One sure way to stay a step ahead of this parenting nightmare is to know and understand the feelings that can grow into burnout. Once you have that knowledge, you become better equipped to deal with your feelings and prevent parenting burnout before it even *thinks* of occurring to you!

Frustration

Is it difficult for you to keep your temper under control when dealing with your toddler? There are a lot of factors at play here, but the primary one is that several parents and caregivers give in to their anger and let themselves spiral out of control. When you allow your toddler to negatively impact your emotions and cause you to lose control, you are giving them the power to dictate how you should behave when, in the right sense, it should be the other way around. Parents and caregivers often respond to their toddlers' behavior without first pausing to reflect. The majority of adults are under the impression that they have an instant responsibility to bring their strong-willed toddler under control, rather than pausing for a moment to consider putting their words and feelings in order before they react. The most effective method to stay in control of your feelings is to figure out what sets you off and to learn to detect the signs that indicate you are about to lose your temper.

Regardless of how laid-back you are, there will come a time when your strong-willed toddler will do something that causes you to feel very upset. If you are unable to remain calm and in control of the situation when your little human upsets you, then you are contributing to the very environment that you are trying to do away with. An excellent example is a scenario in which you are instructing your strong-willed toddler how to play some new game you thought they would like. Your toddler is complaining, being irritable, and talking back to you because they do not understand what you are saying. In another word, inside you, feelings of annoyance, anger, frustration, and disappointment are cooking up, ready to explode. The responsibility of instructing your strong-willed toddler how to play this game lies heavy on both of your shoulders, but still, they refuse to comply. The next step is that you may yell at your sweet little human being, but they continue to fight against your suggestions. After that, it may get even worse due to the fact that they are so anxious that you are distracting them by pouring instructions to them. Their stubborn mind can even go as far as whispering, "It's not as if you cannot figure it out yourself, Tom."

Resultantly, Tom performs poorly because he realizes that you are trying to force him to comply. If we were to translate that directly into the language that Tom and his mind use with each other, it would mean that you are trying to overpower him, and who wants to lose? For that reason, your toddler lets their strong will take charge.

When something like this occurs, rather than losing your cool and responding, ask yourself how you can keep your cool in order to provide the right assistance your toddler needs. Remind yourself that it is not your duty to convince them to play the game; rather, it is your responsibility to maintain your composure and offer proper directions as necessary. From there, you will be able to consider the most efficient approaches to support your free-spirited child in their educational pursuits. In the end, if you let your temper get the best of you and lose control of the situation, you will bring about the very outcome that you have been working so hard to prevent.

Embarrassment

If your spirited toddler tends to misbehave in public, throws temper tantrums, or often displays a disrespectful attitude, you may experience feelings of embarrassment that make you feel out of place when you are with your friends. Strong-willed toddlers acting inappropriately is not new, definitely not with spirited toddlers. Several parents and caregivers experience feelings of humiliation when their tiny human, who should be peaceful, displays unruly behavior or creates a scene. Parents and caregivers feeling that way is usually an emotional reaction to how they think the people around them might judge them. Sometimes you may find that there isn't really something newsworthy that your strong-willed toddler has done, but because the available adult feels as if eyes are on them, they feel like shrinking down underneath the surface to lay low for a while.

If another parent glances at you while your toddler is crying in a public building such as a church, you might get the impression that they are passing judgment on you, that they probably think you are not doing your job well as a parent, or any other crazy ideas, but really, they might just be admiring your bubbly toddler!

The only way to truly know if an onlooker is judging your parenting game is if they come to you and say it to your face. Unless someone has come to you to tell you that you need to take some parenting classes, don't assume they are judging you just because they are looking at you. Here are a few things that can be helpful when you find yourself feeling embarrassed because of your spirited toddler's behavior:

- Pay attention to your surroundings and your toddler. Remind yourself that it is not all about you, and sometimes all it takes is calmly asking your toddler what is wrong with them.
- Keep your attention on the little one, and do not let your eyes wander off them because a lot can happen when you just blink.
- Refrain from defending your parenting styles or making excuses for your tiny one's actions. Instead, you should make straightforward remarks that explain the situation, should you feel compelled to share.
- Instead of reacting to the uncomfortable feeling that you are experiencing, come up with a plan to handle the situation. That will ease your feelings of embarrassment while putting you back in control of the situation.
- If you were visiting someone, had a guest, or any company, make it clear to them that you are addressing the issue, and it is under your control.
- If you need to excuse yourself for a moment, assure the people you were with that you will be in touch later after you handle the business you have with your toddler.
- Give the toddler what they need and refrain from over-explaining your actions or decisions.
- You might feel the need to apologize for your little one's behavior, but unless it is absolutely necessary that you do, refrain from apologizing unnecessarily because that can make you look like a pushover.

Inadequacy

While having a sweet little human with you may cause your heart to fill with love and joy that are almost otherworldly, there will always be instances when their endless questions may sound as though your toddler is determined to annoy you to death. If you are a caregiver, they may complain to you about how much they miss their parents, and if you are their parent covering up for your partner while they attend to something else, your free-spirited toddler may start nagging that you don't take as much good care of them as the other parent. Sometimes our strong-willed toddlers say so many hurtful things one would think they are being paid to get on our nerves, but no. If you are a caregiver, friend, or relative who is just stepping in for the little one's parents, the strong-willed toddler's attitude can make you feel as though you are not enough. Because these little humans prefer to do things their own way, they can easily give off a vibe that they do not need you. This can also be very bad for step-parents and single parents. I mean, what do you tell your spirited toddler if they tell you they would rather be with their other parent?

Parenting a strong-willed toddler can leave you feeling inadequate because they have their way of showing you that they can and will do what they want their way. That is the point at which several parents and caregivers raise their hands to surrender that it is indeed challenging to raise a spirited toddler. Some try and find strategies with which they can stand the chance of turning their little one's head in awe, others give up, and others keep trying the same techniques with the hope that someday their child will change. Will they, though?

Helplessness

Do you have feelings of helplessness on a regular basis when your spirited toddler presents a problem that you are unprepared to handle? It could be that your strong-willed toddler feels sad and irritated, but you have no idea how you can help improve their mood. You may find yourself at a loss regarding how to manage the problem, and that can cause you to feel helpless.

Other factors that might leave you feeling helpless are if your strong-willed toddler is rude to you, slam doors in your face when you try to give them counsel, and if they try and find every excuse to avoid being with you, and many other concerning behaviors of that sort. How are you supposed to know what to do about the behavior if you don't even know why it's happening? It is possible that their unacceptable behavior might continue even if you discipline them, yell, or lovingly give them instructions in a calm manner. As a parent or caregiver, you may find yourself wondering why things are that way with your free-spirited toddler. Failure to identify the main root of that behavior can drain you and leave you feeling powerless because you will not have a solution until you uncover the fueling factors behind the difficulties that you are having with your toddler.

Dear parent, dear caregiver, take a gentle step back, refrain from needlessly condemning your lovely tiny being but draw all your parenting energy into the events that led up to your toddler's unacceptable behavior. As you peruse through those events, keep an eye out for anything you think may have caused your little one to behave the way they are. That can be anything, from their toy malfunctioning to you forcing them to eat lettuce when all they wanted was bacon. Again, remember that it is not always about you. Sometimes the cause of their behavior has nothing to do with what you may or may not have said or done. Sometimes it's just them reacting to the world not working the way they want because, well, the outside world is free-spirited too!

Guilt

A lot of parents and caregivers occasionally experience feelings of guilt. You may have the feeling that you ought to be doing this in a different way. You may feel as though you are not handling situations well or that you have to do better than you already are.

This is a sentiment that a lot of people have, and it is only normal to want to provide the very best for your toddler. The good news is that those difficulties you are experiencing are not new and have not started with you. Although difficult to deal with, what that means is that you can get through that guilt; you can rise above and overcome it. Even though other parents and caregivers don't have it written on their forehead, although they may not always express their parenting struggles, a lot of parents have the same thoughts and feelings. They deal with guilt more often than they may let on.

Consider the circumstances behind your guilt. Ask yourself if the cause is something you can turn around. Think about the approaches you can take to change the course of your parenting journey without pushing yourself over the edge and accomplish those. Accept the fact that feeling guilty is a normal emotion for a parent or caregiver to experience, especially if the circumstances are out of their control. Pinpoint the things, actions, or situations that make you feel guilty the most and deal with those. Trying to overcome your guilt is a waste of energy and can alter how you behave toward other people.

Treat yourself with compassion and understand that you are doing much better than you may believe you are. Reflect on events that make you happy, count the positives and highlight your triumphs, big and small. It's possible that seeing other happy families on social media might make you feel terrible about yourself, but prevent the pressure of social media from getting to you. Keep in mind that most individuals will only publish positive things for the public to see. If you find that limiting your level of social media engagement is helpful, do so and save yourself weeks, months, and years of unjustified guilt.

The Impact of Burnout

Pressure can sometimes be encouraging, but if left uncontrolled, it can become severe and hazardous to your health. It can also have a detrimental influence on your mental, physical and emotional wellbeing. The impacts of stress vary for everyone, but there are certain common concerns that many parents and caregivers who look after strong-willed toddlers may suffer.

Some of the mental, physical, and emotional effects that you may encounter as a result of unaddressed burnout while raising a spirited toddler include:

- low immune function and increased susceptibility to infections and diseases
- decreased energy levels and resultant lack of productivity
- lack of motivation and compromised level of creativity
- sleep-related challenges and the resultant decrease in concentration levels
- irritability, anxiety, or depression
- physical symptoms such as headaches, muscle pains, and dizziness
- digestive and gastrointestinal problems
- mood and appetite fluctuations
- unstable weight gain and loss patterns

When the influence of severe parenting burnout mixes up with additional risk factors such as substance use, parents and caregivers find themselves fighting several other health challenges. Harmful behavior such as reckless drinking or smoking worsens parenting burnout, although you may partake in it to alleviate parenting stress and forget the pain for a while. In the long run, that dangerous mistake eventually catches up with you to claim its debt. You may end up battling problems such as diabetes, obesity, heart disease, sexual dysfunction, and numerous other challenges. If you ignore your parental burnout or its signs, it only gets worse. You do not want the pressure of parenting burnout when dealing with a spirited toddler because the burnout does not only affect your body and mind but your relationship with your strong-willed toddler as well. We will discuss more on this in one of the upcoming sections.

MISTAKES IN PARENTING

Inconsistency

How can you expect your spirited toddler to follow the rules you put in place if you do not model that behavior for them to learn? You need to stick to the rules and restrictions you establish if you want them to stand. If you establish that your little one should wash their face and dress up every morning before they come down for breakfast, see to it that they listen and abide by that rule every day. If they ignore a rule one day and you let it slide, you create an environment for fights the next time you want them to follow the rule. You may confuse their mind into not knowing what is wrong and the opposite, or you may create a situation that makes them want to try ignoring rules to test if you will do anything about it. Once your spirited toddler studies you and graduates, you are done for. Try not to make arrangements that you won't be able to meet. That way, you avoid creating an environment that feeds unhealthy behaviors such as disobedience.

Different Caregivers

One major problem that causes inconsistencies in parenting is sharing the parenting responsibilities with a number of different people every time. While it may sound like a good idea in terms of splitting the burden, each parent or caregiver you leave with your little one has their own concept of how to go about parenting. It does not make much of a difference that you told the person covering for you how they should take care of your toddler because they might still decide to go with what they understand best. A simple example to explain this is if you do not want your strong-willed toddler eating candy except on special occasions when you leave them with someone else. However, the person in charge might decide that a little candy won't hurt if it will stop your spirited toddler from nagging. Your little one, being the smart toddler they are, will most likely use the same nagging tactic next time they have a different person taking care of them. Eventually, they will learn that they can have candy with most of the other adults who take care of them, but when they are with you, they might have to hide and pretend not to eat candy as you instructed. While this might not sound sneaky right now because you are just reading about it, imagine if your innocent toddler started hiding that candy for later consumption. Granny Anna comes and buys the toddler candy to cheer up, and they leave some to eat during bedtime because they know that they should never have candy without your permission. Who then would you blame in that kind of situation? The various Granny Annas that have been helping you, your spirited toddler, or yourself? Whose mess is this?

As if the secrecy is not enough to the damage already, let us zoom into how this inconsistency can even take another step forward and involve you too. Now that your sweet toddler has learned to manipulate adults to get what they want, what would you do if you found a bunch of candy in their pillowcase? Would you beat them, or would you yell? Would you let it slide, or would you confront them? Think about it.

Absent-Mindedness

Many of us are guilty of this one! Remember that night when you returned home after a hard day at work and just wanted to get ready for bed and get some peaceful rest? Good. Now imagine if your little one came to ask you if they could watch another episode of their favorite series, and you absent-mindedly agreed despite it having been way past their bedtime. You were exhausted, of course, no one can crucify you for that, but the long-term implications of not sticking to your own rules can be quite damaging for your relationship with your toddler as well as your overall parenting journey.

Dangers of Inconsistency

Reduced Growth Rate

If you have devised a method that is successful in preventing your strong-willed toddler from wetting the bed, another caregiver may come into the picture and alter certain aspects of the plan. There is a possibility that your toddler will have trouble adjusting to a new strategy that just sprung out of nowhere. Worse yet, by the time you notice there have been modifications to your original plan, your toddler might have already familiarized themself with the new procedure. What that means is that if you want to switch back to your old way of doing things, you have no other way of doing that without restarting from scratch.

Reluctance

Your strong-willed toddler will pick up on the way you parent as they watch you interact with them. If you had trained your spirited toddler to clean up after themself but later decided it is sometimes okay for them to leave dirty bowls of cereal all over the kitchen counter, they might be unwilling to help on the day you actually need them to assist you. We can track the refusal to perform tasks that we expect of our strong-willed toddlers to inconsistency in our parenting strategies.

Loss of Control

When you go to chill with other parents and caregivers, you may have heard some parents complaining that their little ones are very difficult, that their toddlers cannot follow instructions, or many other similar stories. Most of all those times, it all really is just due to inconsistency in their parenting approaches. When you put rules in place for your toddler to follow, you have to make it a point that they follow the rules at all times unless there is a really justifiable reason to deviate. In other words, this basically means that you, as a parent or caregiver, have to follow up on your own rules to make sure your strong-willed toddler follows the guidelines at all times. If you give them free passes every now and then, you may confuse them at first, but eventually, they may learn to dare you. When they realize that your rules are all just talk, they all lose value, and your spirited toddler won't even have to bother following them!

Negligence

You obviously are a decent parent or caregiver who always strives to do a better job, but sometimes a little neglect can seep into your parenting strategies and impact your role as a parent or caregiver in the life and development of your toddler. It is possible to end up being neglectful while trying to avoid overparenting your strong-willed toddler. If you think you may have reduced your involvement in your little one's life, you might want to work on ditching negligence because inattentive parenting poses a threat to both the overall development of your strong-willed toddler and your relationship with them. Neglectful parenting is not always a parent's or caregiver's fault; sometimes, it can be traced back to elements that are beyond our control.

Among the various factors that can cause parents or caregivers to neglect their tiny humans is a lack of resources. A low income can have a bad impact on your strong-willed toddler's development. This is because you will be unable to satisfy your little one's fundamental needs, such as providing them with healthy food choices or encouraging social interaction, if your finances are not in order. When there are few resources available, parents and caregivers have a tendency to become overwhelmed and stressed, and, as a result, they may shift their focus from their little ones. Some parents and caregivers who are unable to manage their responsibilities may even become so frustrated they take their anger and disappointment out on their strong-willed toddlers.

Another problem that fuels negligence in parenting is pure recklessness. It is unfortunate to have to spell it out, but the reality is that not all parents and caregivers are as loving and concerned as you are. Some have major issues being attentive to the needs of their strong-willed toddlers.

In the same manner that negligence has factors that influence it in parents and caregivers, it resultantly causes problems that will manifest in your strong-willed toddler's life if you do not address them on time. One of the problems that result from negligence is your bubbly toddler losing confidence in themself. One major quality that drives your spirited toddler is the faith they have in their abilities. If they lose that confidence, they lose a significant part of what makes them who they are. Lowered confidence levels can have a catastrophic impact on your toddler's entire life. The damage can range from social relationships, academic life, and many other areas of their life.

Neglecting your strong-willed toddler's needs can also slow down their growth in various aspects of life. If you withhold the love and attention that your toddler needs, you may leave them feeling unloved and abandoned. Another problem is that they might miss out on various life experiences, and when the time comes for them to go out into the real world, they find themself lost and unprepared. One of the worst things that can happen in the life of a spirited child is having to depend on other people for almost everything. That is because we are talking about boss toddlers who live for the reins! If you withhold special care and genuine love from your spirited toddler, they might find themself unprepared to deal with the harsh demands of the outside world. That includes making friends, studying on their own, exercising self-control, and much more.

No one has the right parenting formula. All we can do is take steps to right a few wrongs as we go. If you have some negative parenting habits that you now think might disturb your strong-willed toddler's growth, you can take various steps to work on them and become a better caregiver or parent to your strong-willed little one.

TAKING BACK CONTROL OF YOUR EMOTIONS

It is imperative that you seek assistance when the demands of nurturing a strong-willed toddler and running a home as a responsible adult cause you too much pressure and struggle. Here are some different approaches that can assist you in developing your resilience. These are possibilities that center on things that you can do right now from the comfort of your own home. Allow yourself to take steps to lower your stress and increase your happiness in whatever ways you find to be the most effective.

Strategies

Spit Out the Guilt

You should make every effort not to feel bad about spending a little time away from your little human. Finding pleasant and soothing activities that focus on the things you enjoy can help you feel more satisfied and balanced outside your position as a caregiver or parent. Ensure that you stick to activities that focus on things you actually enjoy doing; otherwise, the sacrifice will go to waste. Do not consider spending some of your energy on your happiness to be time-wasting and distracting. Several parents and caregivers tend to feel as though investing effort into their happiness is an unrealistic waste of time, but that is untrue because your overall wellness is at stake here. Your mental health has a significant impact on the mental health of your strong-willed toddler, so it is essential for the health and safety of your precious little one that you take care of yourself first.

Prioritize Personal Time

Reading a book or spending time with friends are both activities that parents and caregivers should make an effort to fit into their schedules on a regular basis, even if it means setting aside only brief periods here and there. Having said that, it can be challenging to find time for yourself, especially if you often tend to be the only adult taking care of your strong-willed toddler. You may ask a friend or relative to watch your toddler while you take a break, or you can let your toddler play their favorite educational games while you unwind with a good book. Do whatever works best for you and the circumstances at hand.

Build a Team

Reach out to friends, relatives, and other people you can find through online support groups. Establishing and nurturing those connections are both great ways for you to construct a social support network as a parent or caregiver. Having others to talk to —people who understand the specific challenges of raising a spirited child—can be quite beneficial. You can also search for single parenting-focused pages and organizations on social media platforms such as Twitter and Facebook. It is possible that linking yourself up with a support team will provide you with an excellent opportunity to connect with other parents and caregivers who have been through situations that are comparable to your own, people who managed to beat parenting burnout and also survived strong-willed toddlers.

Embrace Optimism

You may find yourself focusing a lot of your attention on potential dangers and bad vibes, but that only keeps you from achieving your parenting goals. This worry and pessimism can seep into your interactions with your toddler and worsen the situation. Negative self-talk has a significant impact on your confidence levels as a parent or caregiver. It is also a fatal enemy to your mental well-being. If you want to be a better parent or caregiver, you need to stop talking negatively to yourself. Put out the effort to steer clear of negativity in whatever form, whether it comes from within you or from outside sources.

Set Boundaries

It is essential for you as a parent or caregiver who is raising a strong-willed toddler to establish boundaries around what you can accept and what you will not tolerate. Establish these boundaries with your toddler, partner, friends, relatives, as well as other people from outside your parenting equation. Don't give other individuals the opportunity to waste your time, take you for granted, or take advantage of your efforts. Some people may have their eyes and mouths open, ready to judge the choices you make against the decisions they made when they were in a situation that was similar to yours right now. It is imperative that you make it very clear and direct to those around you that you do not accept or welcome such unfair scrutiny. Setting clear boundaries from the beginning helps prevent you from getting overwhelmed, and that resultantly helps you better manage your time and energy. It will also assist you in achieving an equilibrium between your life as a parent or caregiver and your life as just you.

Burnout Management

Parents and caregivers who are attempting to cope with parenting burnout may find that practicing burnout management techniques is useful. In addition to various methods of relaxation, it is critical to engage in healthy self-care practices and pay close attention to one's mental health.

Make Lifestyle Changes

When you are raising a spirited toddler, you have a lot of responsibilities, and it can be easy to forget about your own health requirements in the midst of all that stress. Healthy eating, regular exercise, and enough rest should be priorities for parents and caregivers who want to make it out of this in good shape. Maintaining your healthy routines even when life gets stressful is one way to guarantee that you are still taking good care of yourself.

Schedule for Relaxation

Incorporating efficient methods of relaxation into your normal routine might also be of great use to you. You can resort to these tactics to unwind and stay on top of stress and pressure when you realize that the day-to-day challenges of raising a strong-willed toddler are starting to work their way toward your demise. A few relaxation tactics you may find helpful include:

- meditation
- deep breathing exercises
- progressive muscle relaxation
- mindfulness
- yoga

Mind Your Mental Well-Being

If your levels of stress are high, you may have a higher risk of experiencing depression, anxiety, and other mental health problems. If you are having trouble sustaining your mental wellness while raising a spirited toddler, you may want to consider seeking assistance from a mental health expert. Therapy groups, counseling, and medication are some of the many options available to parents and caregivers today.

Identify Your Backup Team

If you do not have a solid support system in place, it is easy to find yourself in a position where you are always feeling overwhelmed and on the verge of burning out. You should try to spend as little time as possible around negative people, but at the same time, you should strive to establish a network with as many positive-minded people as you can. Construct a support system for yourself if you do not already have one in place. You can meet other parents and caregivers and make friends through support groups and playdates. Other caregivers and parents are a great source of consolation and information since they have been in your shoes and can empathize with the situation you are dealing with at the moment. They have been where you are and already did what you are learning to do. You can learn from their mistakes and come out even better than they did. You can also share the struggles that you are going through at the moment with your relatives and siblings.

Always Put Yourself First

If you ask the majority of parents and caregivers who they put first in their living setups, many of them might respond that it is their children. However, if you do not take care of yourself, you will not be able to adequately care for anyone else. Always put your own needs first. It does not imply that you are not providing for your toddler or the rest of your family. It does not mean you are not acting in their best interests in any way, shape, or form. It simply indicates that you need to maintain your wellness in order to take care of anyone else. It is not only okay for you to free some time for yourself, but it is also necessary for you to do so in order to avoid reaching a point of exhaustion as a caregiver or parent. If you are interested in trying something new, you may pick up a hobby, find a work-at-home job, or enroll in a class designed specifically for parenting. Those seemingly insignificant activities that you can easily do for yourself have a significant impact on your mental health as well as the ease with which your household functions without the pressure of consistently rising burnout levels.

Chill With Your Partner

There is a good reason why we refer to these people as significant others. Throughout the many stages of parenting that we will go through together, their part also plays a crucial role. Remember to maintain your relationship and keep the fire burning. Make an effort to spend time with your partner every once in a while despite how exhausted you may feel. On the days when you feel emotional exhaustion creeping up on you, having a straightforward chat with your partner every day can provide you with just the emotional boost you need. Constant communication with your partner will improve your outlook on the future. It may be helpful to remind yourself that in the end, you would have had some time to relax and unwind with your significant other, even though the idea might sound unrealistic given your busy schedule.

Let Your Partner Help

When you feel as though parenting has taken you out of the game, your partner can pick you up and assist you in getting back on the playing field. There are many people who wish to assist, but sometimes parents and caregivers are not very welcoming. Some parents and caregivers may act as though they expect the people helping them to do things in the same manner that the caregivers or parents would, but that is unrealistic and unreasonable. No one will ever be able to feed your toddler or teach them to do things exactly the way you would. Different people have different ways of parenting, and every caregiver and parent has to put that fact into consideration before seeking help from others.

Your significant other can be an invaluable resource. Just take a step back and give them space to do what they can for you. It makes no major difference whether your toddler wore red pajamas on Sunday, whereas you would usually dress them in blue ones.

When it comes to providing assistance, it is very simple for parents or different caregivers to disagree. You may change up a few things in and around your home only for your partner to suggest that you could have done it differently.

Watch Your Screen Time

Sometimes, parents allow their digital devices to distract them from paying enough attention to the needs of their toddlers. If you also have a habit of getting lost on your phone or laptop, that is one you have to work on ditching because it harms both your parenting journey and the kind of relationship you have with your strong-willed toddler. Not only does your free-spirited toddler learn bad habits by witnessing you with gadgets in your hands all the time, but you are also causing unnecessary stress for yourself by spending too much time on your device. You are only placing an unreasonable amount of pressure on yourself to be that great parent you see on social media. There is no such thing as the perfect parent, so if you read all those exaggerated Instagram posts hoping to be like one of the so-called flawless parents, give it up already. Keep in mind that not everyone will be totally honest about the experiences they have had as a parent. The majority of your friends probably won't post on social media about the trying days that they had as parents, but you will find loads of flattering pictures and heartwarming videos on their social media timelines. If you have trouble controlling your screen time, try going gadget-free for a few hours a day, and you will realize just how much weight lifts from your shoulders.

Kill the Critic

Several parents and caregivers appear to have a ruthless inner critic that nags them all day and night. Because of this critical voice within, they begin to doubt everything, including how well they are doing their parenting job. This continuous criticism is harmful to the parents or caregivers as well as their tiny humans. If you have this inner critic, it can make you feel as though you are losing your touch as a parent or caregiver. You need to have the courage to tell that inner voice to shut up and get out of your head! You can tell it off because you are doing your job just fine. You are enough. If you're a stay-at-home parent or caregiver, there will be days when you feel like you're barely holding on. However, despite being an excellent caregiver or parent, there are some challenges to parenting that you may find difficult to overcome. That is normal and acceptable. Being a good parent does not mean you should always do everything right. No one does that and survives because it is simply impossible.

Sleep

The exhaustion that results from getting inadequate sleep as a parent or caregiver puts you at risk for parental burnout. Get yourself some peaceful sleep when it is time to rest. Insufficient sleep makes it impossible for you to perform at your best, so all the reasons you may have for starting up at night instead of letting yourself drift into dreamland are not enough. None of the excuses you might come up with will suffice because, in the end, you still won't be able to function once sleep deprivation joins the long list of habits and behaviors that you need to work on. When you factor in your free-spirited toddler, it becomes even clearer that you have a need for adequate rest in order to be a cheerful parent or caregiver who is prepared to face yet another day of arguments, potty training, and many other responsibilities.

Know Your Limits

Don't bother trying to accomplish everything because you simply cannot. It is impossible. You may feel bad about turn people down when they request something of you, but if you turn them down because you know you will not manage to fulfill them, then you should not feel bad about that. You have to be able to recognize when it is appropriate to decline or accept a request because no matter how efficient you may be, you are only one person and cannot do everything at once. Try to restrict the number of tasks you take on to only what you can manage in the given time and always consider your responsibilities as a caregiver or parent. If you don't do this, you will have to prepare for a great deal of parental burnout.

Let Your Toddler Help

There are times when you may find it simpler to carry out tasks for your toddler rather than encouraging them to accomplish things on their own. However, the first step toward encouraging an autonomous child who understands and is ready to show responsibility is to give them opportunities to do things on their own. At first, it might be unfavorable for you to encourage your toddler to make their own cereal because they are most likely to make a mess with the milk and spill the cereal all over your kitchen counter, but it gets better, and honestly, that is exactly what you need when dealing with a strong-willed toddler. You cannot have them tell you they won't eat the cornflakes you made because you made them too soggy, because the next morning, they will tell you the cornflakes are so crunchy the inside of their mouth hurts!

Give your little one space to teach themself how to do some things on their own. That frees up some of your time so you can take a break, but that is not all. It gives your toddler room to grow, and you will realize that they are pleased with their achievement, despite it not being as flawless as it would be if you did it for them. Soon, your spirited toddler will prepare to take on more significant responsibilities. The more responsibility your strong-willed toddler takes on for themself, the less work you will have to do.

Take a Break

You need a break from your parenting duties every once in a while. Find a program that gives parents and caregivers opportunities to mingle during weekends or some other time that suits your schedule. You can also check with a relative you can trust to see if they would be interested in hosting your toddler for a playdate on a regular basis, whether it be for a couple of hours at a time or just once in a while. You can also arrange babysitting turns with other parents whose toddlers get along with your free-spirited toddler. That way, you trade babysitting time with each other, meaning you get some time away from your toddler at no additional cost to you. Perfect, right?

If that does not sit well with you, you can investigate various child care choices that offer both flexibility and reasonable pricing. Be careful not to spend your entire break running errands or doing chores because this is your time off, and you should enjoy it! You deserve a peaceful break.

5

YOUR FEELINGS AND YOUR TODDLER

PARENTING STYLES

Developmental psychologists discovered and studied the connections that lie between child development and the various ways in which parents and caregivers raise their little ones. The developmental psychologist Diana Baumrind analyzed that most parents and caregivers adopt one of the three parenting approaches: authoritarian, authoritative, and permissive parenting. Later, Maccoby and Martin proposed the uninvolved or neglectful parenting style as a fourth approach that some parents tend to exhibit in their ways of parenting. We will only focus on the first three parenting styles before proceeding to positive parenting for the purpose of this book.

Authoritarian Parenting Style

This approach to parenting has very strict regulations by parents and caregivers. Authoritarian parents and caregivers demand flawless compliance from their little ones. In this approach to parenting, there are no exceptions or deviations of any kind for any sort of reason. The consequences that follow if the toddlers in this kind of environment break rules are harsh, and the toddlers have to endure their punishment without asking questions or making excuses. In this parenting approach, the parents or caregivers do not explain why the rules are important; instead, they just demand that their toddlers obey those rules. When it comes to obedience, authoritarian parents have unbelievably high expectations for their toddlers, but they do not provide enough directions on how to do things or improve. If they want their toddler to do something, they will just say what they want, but they have no time or willingness to explain why or how their little one should carry out the given task. They ignore their toddler's requests for clear instructions, sit back and expect the work or result to be mistake-free. It usually becomes quite challenging for the toddlers in this kind of environment to complete some of the assigned tasks with insufficient knowledge of the requirements because they will have no way of knowing what direction to take.

Authoritarian parenting involves little to no feedback because the involved parents and caregivers prioritize compliance without hesitation. When authoritarian parents and caregivers do give their toddlers feedback, they often coat it with critical comments about what the toddler did wrong, completely ignoring what their little one did right. It is progressive to have someone point out what went wrong so a toddler can improve going forward, but that is not how things roll in an authoritarian setting. This parenting approach often substitutes punishment for discipline, with parents and caregivers who lack the ability or desire to justify their policies. That is what fails this parenting style as a strategy you can adopt to raise your little one. Your strong-willed toddler would need to know what they did incorrectly in order to make improvements that will help them do better in the future. The following list includes some traits of this parenting style, contributing variables, and the effects of authoritarian parenting on strong-willed toddlers.

Characteristics of Authoritarian Parenting

According to Baumrind, it is a parent's responsibility to introduce their strong-willed toddler to the norms and values of society, but how much influence a parent has over their free-spirited toddler will primarily determine how well they can accomplish the goal. Authoritarian parenting exhibits the most control over toddlers when compared to other parenting philosophies that we shall explore later in this section. This parenting style exclusively focuses on severe punishment for mistakes rather than constructively teaching toddlers to regulate their behaviors and establish self-discipline. Sometimes the errors that the toddlers in this kind of environment make are too minor to warrant the kind of punishment they receive.

Absence of Warmth

These parents focus so much on good behavior that they neglect their duty to provide opportunities for play and enjoyment. The parents come across as cold, unreasonable, and unloving when they raise their innocent toddlers in such tough settings. Toddlers who grow up in this parenting environment will often make a lot of mistakes because their parents and caregivers do not provide them with adequate explanations regarding the set rules. Instead of encouraging their strong-willed toddlers, authoritarian parents and caregivers may yell or resort to physical punishment such as whipping.

Demanding Tone

There are more rules and regulations in an authoritarian setting than a judge can count. In an effort to manage choices, actions, and relationships, authoritarian parents and caregivers hover over their toddlers' lives. At home, at school, in church, and even in external social settings, authoritarian parents and caregivers often try to micromanage their strong-willed toddlers. They demand straight-forward obedience to orders, yet they are unable to give the necessary information about the directives in question.

Unjustified Penalties

Parents and caregivers who use the authoritarian approach to raising their strong-willed toddlers lack flexibility and patience. They lack the flexibility to explain why their toddlers should or shouldn't do certain things. These parents and caregivers don't realize that by withholding clear instructions and explanations, they might become quite irritated when their strong-willed toddlers struggle with accomplishing tasks or become totally unco-operative. With little to no comprehension of the reasons for the punishment, strong-willed toddlers in authoritarian settings often have to endure unreasonable punishment.

Limited Options

Authoritarian parents and caregivers tend to get overly involved and seek to control all major decisions. They may actively try to control their strong-willed toddler's life, and that becomes a problem because strong-willed toddlers need their freedom. Parents and caregivers in authoritarian settings only understand right and wrong. They leave no room for bargaining or deviations of any kind. Strong-willed toddlers who live with authoritarian parents or caregivers struggle with communication because authoritarian parents and caregivers do not accommodate the idea of their toddler voicing concerns or difficulties.

Mistrust

Authoritarian parents and caregivers give their little one's little independence to explore the world and mature because they don't trust their toddlers to do the right things. They closely watch their strong-willed toddlers to make sure they don't make mistakes, as opposed to fostering decision-making in their toddlers.

Shaming

Authoritarian parents and caregivers often spew embarrassing comments and feedback as their mistaken way to encourage their strong-willed toddlers to improve or get them to follow the rules. These parents and caregivers may insist that they shouldn't have to repeat themselves before their strong-willed toddler grasps something. They may also pass critical remarks such as emphasizing that their little one is unteachable.

Parents and caregivers who impose their preferences on their toddlers usually have factors that influence that behavior. They may or may not know it, but it can be due to their own upbringing as well. If you often use the authoritarian approach to parenting, you may realize that there is a part of you that was raised in an authoritarian environment as well. You may also exhibit a degree of unfriendliness and a lack of empathy in your way of parenting as a result of your own stern outlook on life. A rigid outlook on life can contribute to your struggle to sustain meaningful connections with your free-spirited toddler or with other people around you.

Effects of Authoritarian Parenting

Strong-willed toddlers who grow up with authoritarian parents and caregivers may:

- develop very poor self-esteem because they become used to their parents or caregivers telling them that they cannot do things right when in the actual sense, most of the tasks in question would have been close to impossible to complete.
- exhibit depressive symptoms or develop anxiety due to constantly wondering whether they have met their parent or caregiver's expectations.
- act hesitant in public due to the fear of humiliation since their parents and caregivers sometimes resort to shaming their efforts to encourage what they regard as good behavior.
- lack concern for other people because the whole point of empathy may not exist in their core of being human due to the authoritarian environment lacking empathy itself.
- lack social skills as they may not have had enough social interactions to familiarize themselves with the world outside of the authoritarian environment in which they were raised.
- lack self-control as a result of having been under the control of their parents or caregivers throughout their toddlerhood and early childhood years.
- lose their motivation and self-reliance because they would have become acquainted with failure and being told how unreliable they are.

When exposed to real-life situations in which they have to face the outside world without their parents, strong-willed toddlers who were raised in authoritarian setups may struggle with establishing self-control because they may lack a basic understanding of how boundaries work.

Authoritative Parenting Style

Compared to authoritarian parents, authoritative parents are more democratic. In contrast to the strategy outlined above, authoritative parenting encourages strong-willed toddlers to raise questions when they need additional clarification on certain regulations. Authoritative parents have high expectations for their little ones because they want more for them. The good part here is that parents and caregivers who use this approach are willing to give their tiny humans feedback, support, and encouragement along the road. The parents and caregivers in this kind of environment are eager to talk about any subjects their free-spirited toddlers need help with. They encourage their strong-willed toddlers to work on specific areas that require some improvement. These parents and caregivers also provide detailed feedback when their strong-willed toddlers do well or make mistakes. These kinds of parents and caregivers are kind, agreeable, and understanding when they interact with their little ones and respond to their inquiries. Parents and caregivers who use the authoritative approach manage to keep their eyes on their toddlers' interactions without creating a suffocating environment. Because they want to raise responsible kids who can care for themselves even in the absence of adult supervision, authoritative parents and caregivers encourage discipline and self-control in their strong-willed toddlers. They have realistic expectations and provide adequate collaboration in the execution of the tasks they set for their toddlers, creating a fair and loving environment that also encourages the development of their strong-willed toddlers.

Some of the traits of this kind of parenting approach include:

- promoting the right to free expression such that the strong-willed toddlers involved can voice their concerns without fear of punishment or embarrassment
- valuing the opinions that the strong-willed toddlers involved may have when discussing solutions for important issues in the family or other decisions that involve the little ones
- setting clear boundaries, outlining fair repercussions, and establishing attainable objectives to encourage the involved toddlers to learn without fear and aim high without intimidation
- fostering self-reliance and decision-making abilities in strong-willed toddlers to help them be able to live their lives without completely relying on their parents for everything later in life
- enforcing consistent and fair consequences for wrongdoings to correct strong-willed toddlers and keep them from making the same mistakes over and over while also helping them become responsible for their mistakes in the future
- showing warmth and unwavering affection and paying attention to their strong-willed toddlers' needs even if the toddlers fail to attain their set goals

Authoritative parenting style is effective because the strong-willed toddlers it produces are composed, orderly, and content. They develop self-control because their parents and caregivers provide positive learning environments that support their strong-willed toddler's development of boundaries. Strong-willed toddlers who grow up in this kind of parenting environment also have a strong belief in their own capacity to perform tasks. That is because the parents and caregivers involved nurture their strong-willed toddlers to develop self-confidence by encouraging them to aim high while still being there for them if they fail. The feeling of knowing that their parents and caregivers still see them the same even when they make mistakes fuels the strong-willed toddlers in authoritative environments to do even better to make the adults around them proud.

Parents and caregivers who use the authoritative approach to raise their strong-willed toddlers are flexible. They do not have rigid expectations, so they can change what they expect of their little ones in response to the situation at hand. When strong-willed toddlers in an authoritative environment make mistakes, their parents and caregivers evaluate the issue and take into account all relevant circumstances that may have contributed to failure before determining the best course of action. These kinds of parents or caregivers are not ashamed to admit mistakes, even if they think they may have contributed to their strong-willed toddler's failure.

The Benefits of Authoritative Parenting

In authoritative environments, parents and caregivers set an example by modeling the behaviors they wish their kids to adopt. The strong-willed toddlers in authoritative environments have such fantastic role models in their lives that they adopt positive behaviors and make it a point to meet their expectations of their adults. They receive reliable standards for what is acceptable and what is not through the regular disciplinary techniques utilized in authoritative parenting. These strong-willed toddlers will continue to treasure the capacity to distinguish good from wrong even as they grow.

Authoritative parents and caregivers encourage their strong-willed toddlers to build on their creativity, maturity, problem-solving skills, and critical thinking. These little ones learn to control their emotions, comprehend what they are saying, and consider the impact of their words and behaviors on those around them. Strong-willed toddlers who are raised by authoritative parents develop some degree of independence because they learn to do things on their own. That encourages the toddlers to test their limits while completing daring activities on their own and laying the groundwork for further growth in self-confidence and self-esteem.

These parenting strategies have their roots somewhere in each parent's background, as was previously said. Some parents naturally utilize authoritative techniques, while others automatically adopt an authoritarian strategy, while others are compelled to adopt a permissive strategy. On the brighter side, though, even if forcing your spirited toddler to do things the way you want is all you have ever known, you can still embrace a more positive approach to parenting and become the best parent you can be.

Permissive Parenting Style

This parenting is also referred to as indulgent parenting. It is characterized by relatively low expectations and little to no punishment. The parents and caregivers in this kind of parenting environment are extremely forgiving and ask very little of their toddlers. Permissive parents and caregivers try their best to avoid conflict, so if they analyze their situation and conclude that confrontation might result in a misunderstanding, they will most likely let the problem slide or deal with it themselves. An easy example that explains this is if your strong-willed toddler left their clothes scattered on the floor because they were rushing to follow someone to the park or mall, but you enter their bedroom before they leave and realize what a mess they made. If you are a permissive parent or caregiver, you might just pick up your little one's dirty clothes and put them where they should be because you would have calculated that telling them to tidy their room up before they leave might make them cry since they are racing against time to join the person who is going out.

Despite being receptive, permissive parents and caregivers do not encourage any sense of restraint or overall maturity in their strong-willed toddlers. Permissive parents and caregivers tend to play the parts of friends with no desire to exert control over their free-spirited toddlers. Permissive parents and caregivers foster a laid-back environment for their strong-willed toddlers, and that stunts the toddler's growth. Mastering self-control and finding a sense of balance in life are some of the main challenges that haunt strong-willed toddlers who grow up with permissive parents or caregivers. The strong-willed toddlers who grow up in permissive parenting environments fail to master important life qualities because their parents and caregivers mistakenly believe that their strong-willed toddlers should exercise the freedom to develop without parental interference.

The following list of traits can help you determine whether or not you might be a permissive parent or caregiver. Parents and caregivers who raise their strong-willed toddlers in this kind of environment often:

- show unlimited kindness, empathy, and devotion to their little ones.
- set a few clear guidelines for what they regard as appropriate conduct.
- allow their strong-willed toddlers to share opinions and actively participate in important decisions.
- focus more on their toddlers' freedom and happiness than their maturity.
- behave more like friends than parents or caregivers.
- reward good behavior to encourage their strong-willed toddlers to follow rules or aim higher.

The Impact of Permissive Parenting

This overly tolerant style of parenting leads to some undesirable behaviors. Due to a lack of guidance in their upbringing, the strong-willed toddlers who are raised in permissive situations lack social skills and are unable to manage themselves. These toddlers may end up with reduced success rates because of their parents' and caregivers' low expectations of them. The little ones raised in permissive environments lose motivation and almost have no goals to strive for because their parents and caregivers provide for them and even do some tasks for them, leaving the tiny humans with little to no room to learn. Strong-willed toddlers from permissive parenting environments also have a tendency to make poor decisions because their parents and caregivers have no problem deciding for them. This causes the toddlers to suffer serious difficulties when confronted with circumstances that require them to make decisions and resolve real-world problems. Another disadvantage of permissive parenting is that without proper advice regarding right and wrong, some strong-willed toddlers may grow up to commit crimes and engage in inappropriate activities. These strong-willed toddlers may also misbehave frequently because of their lack of discernment between right and wrong.

Aggression

The strong-willed toddlers who grow up in permissive environments may not know how to respond to emotionally demanding situations because they don't generally understand their emotions. These strong-willed toddlers may react with hostility when they don't get their way or may be reluctant to help out in the house if there is nothing in it for them.

Lack of Time Management

The strong-willed toddlers from permissive parenting environments may get carried away with leisure pursuits such as gaming and watching television because they lack constant control and discipline. This overinvolvement in leisure wastes their time on useless activities because the toddlers lack basic time management skills. Strong-willed toddlers who are raised in permissive home setups may act out at home and pay little to no attention to rules and regulations.

Remedying Approaches

If you agree that the authoritarian style of parenting is the winner, you might want to implement some of the techniques into your own parenting style. The good news is that you can easily achieve that if you set clear boundaries and are consistent in your strategies, rules, and principles when raising your spirited toddler. Although being more rigorous with your little one may seem like a betrayal of their trust, this is your best shot at ensuring a good future for them. If, for example, you have always been permissive with your spirited toddler, things can turn ugly when you make up your mind to switch things up to parenting with some authority. That, however, does not kill the dream, so you can just get ready to deal with their rage for a while. You will need to establish a set of guidelines to help your spirited toddler cope with the sudden but positive change, as well as help yourself stick to the plan instead of giving up after a few days. Here are some suggestions to assist you through this.

Establish House Rules

Make a list of dos and don'ts for your spirited toddler to abide by. The problem that several parents and caregivers encounter at this point is establishing rules that their spirited toddler still won't follow. You have to remember that when deciding on these rules, your spirited toddler does not appreciate being told what to and what not to do. Let it sink in that your tiny human is not an average toddler and would not survive an authoritarian kind of environment without creating a mini hell for their parents or caregivers. In a harsh environment such as the authoritarian parenting approach, your toddler would easily feel overwhelmed, but to survive, they would also have to exhaust their parents or caregivers. In an authoritative-approach-based environment, however, our toddler might still have difficulties with adjusting but here you can easily outsmart them. Invite your strong-willed toddler to help you decide what rules your household will follow. When you finish setting the rules, have them promise you that they will stick to the rules until you modify them. Once you make that pact with your strong-willed toddler, you have won a contract. Remember that they value their integrity so they will most likely follow the household rules you discussed if that means they retain a sense of dependability.

Once you have solid house rules in place, your toddler will be aware of your expectations and be able to always turn to the rules for guidance. You get them to follow the rules they participated in making, and they get to keep their integrity as someone who does not go back on their word. Both parties win!

Take Action

Many parents and caregivers struggle to follow through to make sure that their strong-willed toddlers accomplish everything in a timely manner and as expected of them. However, by explaining the benefits of adhering to the rules, you encourage your spirited toddler to follow these rules.

Focus on Change

Make sure your strong-willed toddler knows the price for disobedience and that you really mean it when you say it. Keep your promises if they disobey the rules rather than just telling them what would happen if they do not comply. That is because your strong-willed toddler, although you might not know it, is constantly studying the people and other factors around them. Be firm with the rules while you remain loving. Avoid imposing too severe penalties, and keep your requests reasonable.

If you follow these simple remedies to try and adopt a more nurturing approach to raising your strong-willed toddler, you draw steps toward positive parenting.

Positive Parenting

Positive parenting emphasizes the importance of you showing your toddler some degree of respect and them doing the same. This approach revolves around the idea that your toddler does not necessarily get out of bed to get on your nerves. When you practice positive parenting, you focus on encouraging your toddler to develop good habits rather than punishing them for unacceptable behaviors they may have shown in the past. With positive parenting, you use firm but warm techniques to guide your strong-willed toddler on the road to positive development. When you take the positive approach to raising your strong-willed toddler, you create an atmosphere that favors the happiness of your toddler, and when your toddler is happy, you become happy too.

Positive parenting provides an environment that promotes good emotional growth for your toddler because of the parental involvement and warmth it calls for. If you use positive parenting to nurture your strong-willed toddler, you increase the chances of raising a well-behaved little human who is aware of themself as well as their environment, people around them, and how their actions may affect others.

Strong-willed toddlers raised in positive parenting environments have better self-esteem than those who grow up in harsh environments. Your spirited toddler will most likely believe in their ability to carry out activities that their fellow toddlers can. And your bonus—they may even go a step further than the average toddler because of their high level of resilience and heightened ambition.

Because positive caregivers and parents do not feel compelled to punish their strong-willed toddlers to correct unacceptable behaviors, positive parenting also ensures a close relationship between toddlers and the people who take care of them. Positive parenting has no room for hostility, power struggles, yelling, or any other aspects of harsh or neglectful parenting. When you train yourself to communicate with your strong-willed toddler in a calm manner regardless of the circumstances, you create a positive atmosphere for open communication and mutual respect.

When deciding on the consequences of breaking the rules and ignoring direct instructions, try to explain them to your toddler before enforcing them. This gives your toddler a chance to voice their concerns and ask questions where they need clarification. Once that part is clear, see to it that you follow through on the consequences you set. Otherwise, you leave potholes for confusion and encourage your strong-willed toddler to test limits.

When your strong-willed toddler misbehaves, try to focus on why they did what they did. Sometimes their behavior makes sense in their mind, and punishing them without knowing or understanding their side of the misconduct does not help your situation. Once you know why your toddler acted the way they did, you can take a direct approach to address the problem. That will help your toddler feel acknowledged, and even if they don't get their way in the end, they won't feel the urge to misbehave for attention.

6

FORWARD-THINKING ACTION

You have learned different approaches to parenting as well as how to avoid burnout, but what exactly is your next move in this parenting game? Several parents and caregivers seek solutions for their parenting difficulties from time to time, but only a few devise forward-thinking plans. Fortunately, you are one of the few parents and caregivers who seek to identify major areas of difficulty in their parenting strategies for the parenting journey as a whole. You are one of the few who plan solutions in advance. That is what this chapter is about. In this chapter, you will learn to navigate and survive parenting issues that many parents and caregivers face. You will also acquire the basic knowledge necessary to stay ahead of your parenting problems.

ADDRESSING DIFFICULTIES

This is a how-to section with practical hacks and strategies for dealing with some of the difficult scenarios that arise when raising strong-willed toddlers. We will discuss how best you can approach situations such as tantrums, mealtimes, and bedtime, as well as managing your toddler's social interactions and hygiene. From there, you will learn how to encourage good behavior from your spirited toddler without coming off as a difficult parent or caregiver.

Tantrums

Strong-willed toddlers may often throw tantrums that leave you second-guessing your abilities as a parent or caregiver. They are an undeniably normal part of toddlerhood, but tantrums can be quite disturbing at times. When your spirited toddler is in the throes of a temper tantrum, it can be difficult to contain your own emotions, and you might even find yourself exploding back too. Temper tantrums can also be embarrassing in public or when your toddler stages one in front of your friends or colleagues. It is difficult for your strong-willed toddler to cope with situations or accept things that seem to oppose their preference, and that is usually how temper tantrums brew. It is imperative that you get to the bottom of the problem if your tiny human throws tantrums often. Once you uncover what is fueling your toddler's tantrums, you can then adopt approaches to deal with them.

Causes

Temper tantrums often stem from one general cause, and that is your toddler not having their way. Your toddler may throw a tantrum as a way of communicating what they need, such as a change of clothes or diaper, their stuck toy, more milk, and many other things they may need. If you remember the developmental theories we discussed earlier, you may recall that your toddler is building on the abilities they had at birth, but they have not yet acquired verbal abilities to ask for more milk or the motor skills to retrieve their stuck toy from underneath their bed. You must be thinking: Okay, if that is why my bundle of joy acts out sometimes, it's not a big deal. If you are thinking that it will be as easy as changing their diaper every time they cry, you are a little on the wrong side of our story. See, the issue becomes tricky when you have to learn what each cry means because not all the tantrums they will throw serve to request more milk. Sometimes they feel sleepy, other times they feel too cold, and in the loveliest instances, they just want to feel your embrace. It is important to learn how you can properly tell what your toddler wants or needs when they try to communicate because if you misread their signals, it will drive them crazy and send havoc breaking loose.

As your spirited toddler grows, they learn to communicate their needs in a better language than crying, but that does not mean that they will no longer throw tantrums. Despite having a few language skills, your toddler still lacks the ability to control their feelings, so even a minor misunderstanding between them and their toy can fuel a heated fight. Because your strong-willed toddler places high importance on exercising their independence, they are likely to experience increased levels of frustration whenever they need assistance. Your toddler might lose their temper when trying to do something on their own, then discover that they are unable to do it on their own.

It is important to keep in mind that your spirited toddler's fits are not an indication of poor parenting; rather, they constitute a necessary developmental step because it is by things not going your toddler's way that they learn to cope with their negative feelings and live through them. While finding the cause of your toddler's tantrums may be simple, the fix is a little far from easy because you cannot just let them have their way to prevent them from acting out.

Addressing Temper Tantrums

What do you do if your toddler throws a fit, protesting that they do not want to wear a jacket because it might spoil their outfit? Do you give in, yell, beg, or do you bribe them with a golden promise to buy them candy if they just wear the jacket? Despite there being a variety of tactics that parents and caregivers use when dealing with toddler tantrums, only some are effective.

Spanking and yelling are very popular among several parents and caregivers, but they top the list of approaches that DO NOT WORK. Other parents and caregivers choose a gentler road and resort to strategies such as bribery, giving in, or begging and pleading. Bribing your strong-willed toddler to behave may work at that moment, but it encourages them to keep misbehaving because you are basically rewarding their bad behavior with a favorable outcome. If your toddler realizes that you always offer to buy them ice cream whenever they refuse to have their breakfast, ice cream becomes the only way to get them to open their cute mouths and feed. If you beg or give in to your spirited toddler's demands, you are not only praising their behavior but also creating an atmosphere that favors the recurrence of that bad behavior. Pleading with your toddler as a way to get them to do what they should or vice versa strips authority off of you and puts them in a position of power.

Aim to make your no a serious no whenever you deal with your strong-willed toddler. When you respond to your toddler's fits with composure and consistency, you draw firm boundaries they can follow. Consistency helps your toddler feel more secure, but most importantly for a strong-willed toddler, understanding set boundaries make them feel more in control of their situations than when things just change without notice.

When counseling your spirited toddler regarding unacceptable behaviors, you need to emphasize their unacceptable behavior without attacking their emotions. Knowing what it is about their conduct that is unacceptable will help them work on regulating their emotions and improving their behavior. Attacking their feelings, on the other hand, makes them feel misunderstood, inadequate, unloved, insecure, and several other negative emotions. The summation of all those negative feelings can cause your toddler to engage in even worse outbursts or withdraw from you.

Avoid Yelling

Kids learn pretty quickly, so if you have a habit of yelling and barking orders at the top of your voice, your spirited toddler will pick a thing or two from that behavior, and before you know it, you will be exchanging heated outbursts!

Keep in mind that your reaction to situations and how you control your anger shape how your toddler deals with their rage as well. If you often yell at them, they might eventually yell in response to your yelling. Concentrating on how the frustrating situation at hand affects your toddler's emotions can help you keep calm when they are acting out. In some instances, shouting at your toddler could be inevitable. If you realize you are losing your tone while addressing your toddler's challenges, you can apologize to them and start afresh. That way, you reinforce friendly communication, encourage them to own up to their mistakes, and of course, prepare them to give second chances.

Prepare Your Toddler

You may benefit from letting your toddler know in advance if there are going to be any changes in your current or usual setup. This applies to changes in their diet, changes regarding an event you want to attend in the future, changes in your living arrangements, and several other modifications of that nature. When you prepare your spirited toddler for what's to come, you are less likely to have challenges when the time for that change comes. A situation that demonstrates the importance of preparing your toddler in advance is if their cousin was visiting for summer and they had to share their room. You would want to warn your toddler and discuss that in advance to avoid them putting up a show when the whole house is full of visitors. If you have taken your toddler out to have some fun but are having trouble figuring out how to tell them it's time to go home without provoking their outbursts, you can say something like, "We are about to leave. Would you like an ice cream before we go home?" Before you ask, that is not bribery; you are just giving your toddler an opportunity to choose ice cream or just go home. They cannot tell you not to go home when it's time to, but at least they can decide if they would like ice cream before leaving. Eventually, your toddler starts to understand that they can control some things, but others are just beyond their authority. Knowing what's to come comforts them and helps them feel in control because it gives them time to organize their stuff and create space to accommodate the necessary changes.

Address Unacceptable Behaviors Immediately

If your toddler reacts to situations with violence, if they tend to throw, hit, or tear things when they get upset, you have to stop them right away. If they display signs of aggression in a place with other people, such as a game store, you might handle the situation better by first getting them out of the crowded environment. Once you are clear of uninvolved individuals, you can then make it clear that destroying items or hurting others just because things won't go their way is unacceptable.

Spell out what they can and what they cannot do when they are enraged. You can tell them that getting upset is okay, but it does not give them a right to misbehave or act in an aggressive manner.

That sets boundaries and ensures you retain the power to control the situation while helping your toddler feel understood.

Let Your Toddler Feel

Sometimes it is important that your strong-willed toddler expresses their emotions. If they get furious because their toy is not cooperating, allow them to feel the frustration and deal with their rage. You can support them during that time by removing anything dangerous around them, explaining why their toy won't cooperate and suggesting what they can do about their situation. You can also stand by them to provide reassurance and help them feel safe. That teaches your toddler to deal with issues in a constructive manner rather than bottling up their anger only so it can return to haunt them in the future. Allowing your toddler to express their emotions helps them regain composure without losing their temper or causing you to lose yours.

When your strong-willed toddler acts out, remember that they are mostly trying to communicate something, not that they want to embarrass you or fight you. Once you understand they are trying to communicate, you gain the drive to decrypt their message and, as a result, solve the problem without getting yourself all stressed out.

Meals

One other major problem that may arise when raising a strong-willed toddler is managing meals. During toddlerhood, your little one builds their sense of direction, self-control, and communication skills. This is the point at which they discover what foods work best for their taste buds as well as learn to control how much they eat at a time. You may have challenges picking the right meals for your toddler or may find it difficult to get them to follow regular mealtimes. You can help your strong-willed toddler exercise some degree of authority by allowing them a certain level of flexibility regarding what and how much they eat during each meal time. Be careful not to become entirely permissive because your toddler is, after all, just a toddler. They need your guidance to eat healthy foods at regular times and in healthy amounts. Your toddler is still far from deciding and preparing lunch, but you can involve them in the decision-making by asking for their input. You can ask them if, for example, they would like garlic or if you should skip it. If your toddler suggests that you leave out a major ingredient or something very nutritious and important to that dish, you can simply explain to them why you cannot leave that ingredient out, and they will understand. Involving your spirited toddler prevents you from making a dish they won't eat but more importantly than that, knowing their input matters gives your toddler comfort and boosts their confidence.

Another problem that parents and caregivers face when feeding strong-willed toddlers is getting the serving sizes right. Your toddler might eat very little food sometimes, while on other days, they may eat so much you end up worrying about them. Some of the factors that determine how much your toddler eats include:

- the level of social engagement they have with their friends or those around them
- the amount of energy they spend on other activities
- the type of food in question
- distractions during or prior to meal times
- the need to independently determine when and how much they eat

Appetite fluctuations are a common ordeal when raising strong-willed toddlers. One day they love spinach, and the next day even your story about spinach making them intelligent doesn't work.

Once you determine the key factor interfering with your toddler's appetite, you can then channel your parenting energy and skills into resolving the problem. As you try to fix appetite issues in your strong-willed toddler, refrain from forcing them to eat what and when they do not want. Using force will only give your toddler a negative impression of mealtimes, and their behavior might worsen that way.

If your toddler is having trouble finishing their meals, you might also want to revise the amount of food you are serving them in one go. Toddlers have small stomachs and a lot going on in their play lives, so it is normal for your little one to only eat small servings. As long as you can see that your toddler is developing as they should and you provide them with healthy food options, you can trust them to judge how much they eat at each sitting. Their mechanism won't let them starve, and if you offer the right foods in the right portions, malnutrition will never know your toddler's name! If the amount of food your toddler eats in a day worries you, you can squeeze some healthy snacks onto their diet plan. Snacks will give your spirited toddler energy to go about their day without trading their power or forcing themself to eat more than they can handle.

Sometimes the food you offer just isn't the food for your toddler's taste buds. It's essential that your toddler eats what they like as long as it is healthy because that is the only way they can enjoy eating. The good thing is that for almost every healthy food your little one dislikes, there is a close alternative that is just as healthy! Experiment with different foods that offer a similar range of nutrients to see what gets along with your toddler's tastebuds the most. Another tissue with food and strong-willed toddlers is how you cook or serve the food. They may not like their potatoes mashed, or they may prefer their eggs yolkless. If it's important to you that they eat the yolk, for example, you can talk to them about how eating yolk benefits them and why it's important to you that they tap into those advantages.

Try and create a positive atmosphere during mealtimes. Refrain from arguing or discussing misunderstandings when it's time to eat. If difficult conversations are inevitable during mealtimes, you can excuse yourself and finish the conversation outside your toddler's hearing distance. Eating together should be an enjoyable family ritual, a chance to bond while sharing happy meals. A positive eating environment gives your toddler a sense of security and motivates them to eat as much as they can. Sometimes all it takes is your toddler realizing that you enjoy the food too. This is especially true when you are trying to introduce new foods to your toddler's diet. If they see that you don't even enjoy the food in question yourself, they might lose the zeal to try it. Refrain from bribing your toddler with unhealthy treats in an effort to get them to eat healthy foods. If you bribe your toddler to eat healthy meals, it will work that day—and the next—but it won't work how you intended. The candy or whatever currency you would have used to buy your toddler's cooperation becomes the only motive for them eating, and without that, you would have trouble getting them to eat anything.

If your toddler always distracts themself when eating, you can set specific times for their meals and give them a limit on how many minutes they can spend on their meal. When that time elapses, you clear their table, and they have to wait for the next mealtime. This method is not in any way a punishment. It teaches your toddler to respect and adhere to schedules. It helps your toddler understand that each activity has its time. Once they get that in their cute brains, they will respect mealtimes and know to leave their toy when it's time to eat.

You have to be a little more patient with younger toddlers than those who have acquired most toddlerhood abilities. Younger ones are still learning to eat and will make a mess several times. If your toddler is still learning to eat, they might lick their food before eating or just lick and leave it. Several parents and caregivers do not appreciate their toddlers touching, sniffing, or licking food, but that is how your toddler learns what they need to know about the food. They need to explore the taste, aroma, and texture of the food before they develop an understanding of what foods they like most and so on. If your toddler was thrilled about lunch but loses interest after sniffing the food, you can take the food away and try to determine what aroma they did not like. If you can change something about that dish, then you may do so and try again another time. Once you find something your toddler enjoys, switch it up to include a wide variety of nutrients. If they seem to enjoy smoothies, throw in a bunch of fruits and vegetables that blend well and see if your toddler likes the variation.

Your strong-willed toddler may display unfavorable eating habits such as being overly selective, but once you pinpoint the problem they have with the food in question, you graduate from meal challenges with flying colors. You are the one who would start sharing hacks and tips with other parents and caregivers, reassuring them that managing meals is not as difficult as they may think.

Bedtime

Putting toddlers to bed can be as easy as getting meat from a vegetarian friend for some parents and caregivers, but it can be a little different with strong-willed toddlers. Just when you are done with the infancy stage of parenting, thinking you can now rest at night because your baby is grown up, you may realize you actually have more work now. Your strong-willed toddler can oppose going to bed, and sometimes, when you put them to sleep, they may wake up a few minutes later claiming they can't sleep. This can even happen around midnight when you are deep in dreamland.

You can also find that your strong-willed toddler does not want to be away from you at night. There are plenty of problems that you may run into as far as bedtime is concerned in relation to raising your strong-willed toddler. Let us take a brief look at some of the common bedtime problems with strong-willed toddlers and how you can go about them.

Bedtime Delays

Remember that your strong-willed toddler is learning to master their independence and will take advantage of any chance to exercise that power. Therefore, you shouldn't be surprised if your strong-willed toddler tries to delay their bedtime by saying just about anything, even if they are evidently sleepy. When it comes to delaying bedtime, strong-willed toddlers can be crafty. They may ask you to read them another bedtime story, request some food, or take a long break to use the bathroom. They can come up with several kinds of excuses—anything at all to put off having to say good night.

What you can do:

Try making a few tweaks to the bedtime routine your toddler follows. Make sure that your routine has space for the fundamentals, which include giving your little one a bath, reading them a story, hugging them, and finally turning off the lights. As you draw that bedtime schedule for your spirited toddler, you should try to give them opportunities to exercise some freedom along the way. If you give your toddler a chance to choose how or when they sleep before bedtime, they will be less likely to fight it when the time comes. You can start by something as simple as asking them how they want to sleep or what they want to wear to sleep. When your strong-willed toddler knows they had a say when you were planning their bedtime routine, they are more likely to cooperate because then, they won't feel as if you are trying to dictate their life.

Aversion to Darkness

If your toddler dislikes or is afraid of the dark, you may find that their imagination runs wild with all sorts of chilling scenarios, from scary shadows on walls to terrifying monsters hiding under the bed as soon as the lights go out or they wake up in a dark room. While it is common for toddlers to dislike the dark here and there, a serious aversion to the dark can interfere with your strong-willed toddler's nighttime routine.

What you can do:

Your toddler will experience very real emotions in response to their fear of the dark. You can help your strong-willed toddler overcome their aversion to the dark by being in their room. When they see that the dark does not bother you, they will have more peace of mind and can then sleep better knowing you have their back. By simply asking your toddler about the things they are afraid of, you can make a difference in lowering their level of anxiety. Therefore, before you say goodnight to your toddler, try to make them feel more assured, just like you do when they have nightmares. Before turning in for the night, you can distract them from terrifying thoughts by having them do something such as counting their fingers while a nightlight is on. Make an effort to stick as closely as you can to the routine your toddler follows every night. Maintaining the same sleep time schedule reduces the chances of your little one waking up in the middle of the night and probably getting paranoid because of the dark.

Bad Dreams

If your strong-willed toddler cries himself awake in the middle of the night or very early in the morning, he's likely having a nightmare. Nightmares typically occur during REM sleep in toddlers, also known as light sleep. During that time, your little one's brain processes everything that took place throughout the day, including some frightening experiences, such as tv scenes.

What you can do:

Your strong-willed toddler will likely have difficulty distinguishing their dreams from reality, and they may struggle to explain to you what exactly scared them. You can try to reassure your toddler by telling them that it was just their imagination playing tricks on them. You can take your support a step further by joining them in their bed and cuddling them until they fall asleep. You being there gives your strong-willed toddler some assurance and a feeling of safety.

Getting out of Bed

To make the most of their newly found independence, your strong-willed toddler can choose to walk around in their room at odd hours, such as the middle of the night or the wee hours of the morning. They can also take a short stroll to your bedroom or their siblings'.

What you can do:

You can offer to walk your toddler back to their own room whenever they visit yours during bedtime. If you allow them to sleep in your room, you are signing up for an endless cycle of conflict when you are ready for bed, but they still want to play. The same applies if your spirited toddler tends to visit other rooms during bedtime or when they fail to sleep.

Sleepwalking and Sleep Talking

It can be unsettling if your toddler starts mumbling and chatting to themselves while alone in bed or if they start wandering the hallways with their eyes closed in sleep. However, sleepwalking and talking during toddlerhood are quite common, despite the fact that both of these behaviors may be an indication of stress or a lack of sleep.

What you can do:

Unfortunately, as your toddler grows, you will realize there isn't much you can do about either of these situations. Try to make bedtime a relaxing experience for your strong-willed toddler and watch to see that they get enough rest. Also, make sure your house is safe and friendly for your toddler. Try and childproof the house as much as you can, locking all your cabinets, securing all the cables in the house, and clearing any toys or other items that may cause someone to trip and fall. If you find your toddler wandering around the house while in their sleep, you can calmly lead them back to bed instead of trying to wake them up because that can be confusing.

Hygiene

During toddlerhood, your little one is constantly seeking independence to do things on their own, and that is what makes this stage a fundamental stage to introduce hygiene to your toddler. Good hygiene practice can prevent diseases and, of course, will help your toddler to carry themself in a modest way in society. Teaching your strong-willed toddler good hygiene practice is nowhere close to a lazy walk in the park, but with repeated exposure and consistency, your eager-to-learn toddler will soon get the hang of it, and it will eventually become part of their routine.

Toilet Training

Who doesn't want their toddler to master the potty? Toilet training is a developmental milestone every parent would want for their child to achieve. A toddler who knows to carry themself to the bathroom, help themself and flush afterward is the perfect dream in the parenting world. Training your strong-willed toddler to acquaint themself with toilet training will save you from piles of mess, embarrassment, and many other negative situations.

Every toddler is different, and when it comes to the major potty question, the when, there is no single time that suits all toddlers. Because your strong-willed toddler is curious and relentless, they might master toilet training faster than the average toddler. Sometimes, though, your little one might need more time to learn, so you have to exercise patience and look out for signs that indicate your toddler might be ready for toilet training. These signs can manifest between 18 to 24 months, but sometimes you won't recognize them until later.

Some of the indications that your toddler might be ready for toilet training include:

- demonstrating genuine interest in learning to use the potty
- comprehending and employing the language of toilet use, such as knowing to communicate when they need to use the bathroom
- being able to keep their diaper dry for two hours or more

- obeying basic directions such as being told to go to the potty
- waking up with a dry diaper after a long nap
- understanding the difference between the urge to poop and that to urinate

Potty-training a strong-willed toddler is not a one-day job—it takes time and dedication. Some toddlers are quick to learn, but others may need longer than 3 to 6 months. You can get your toddler ready for their potty time by familiarizing each other with names to describe their toilet visits. Several parents and caregivers use words such as peeing and pooping when referring to urinating and defecating, respectively, but you can make it fancy and special by coming up with your own codes that you can even use in public without your toddler feeling embarrassed or anything.

Invest in a comfortable potty for your toddler to use during their toilet training. Your toddler might start off sitting on their clothes or diapers at first, but they will eventually sit on their potty without underwear when they are ready. Once you have determined that your strong-willed toddler is mature enough to start learning how to use the toilet, make sure you have enough time for the actual training. You can demonstrate to your toddler how they should sit on the toilet and explain the process to them, so they have a clear picture. Establish a regular pattern. For instance, if your toddler wakes up in the morning with a dry diaper or an hour after consuming a significant amount of water or juice, consider taking or sending them to the potty. If they sit there and nothing happens, allow them to get up when they want because only they can feel what's going on in their body.

Creating a Game-Like Atmosphere

Strong-willed or not, toddlers love games. When you take

advantage of that and turn it around to work for you, you realize that implementing a game-like atmosphere to help solve your parenting difficulties works like a charm! This method works in most of the tricky situations that parents and caregivers of strong-willed toddlers usually find themselves in. From eating challenges, toys, study time, bathing, and many other situations you can think of, establishing a game-like environment is a mega-hit! Let's explore how best you can use this magic to solve some of your parenting challenges.

If your strong-willed toddler continuously has challenges when playing with other toddlers because they would rather be alone, you can come up with an idea to encourage them to make more friends. Strong-willed toddlers love winning—it's one of the qualities that drive them. Imagine a family event setup where there are several other toddlers. You can challenge your little one to make new friends so you can compare who has the most friends. Chances are your toddler will have lots of friends to introduce to you by the time the event ends.

If your strong-willed toddler has a tendency to leave their toys scattered all over, you can devise a game that requires them to tidy up their space. To make it even more interesting, you can have them compete against the way you tidy your bedroom, have them finish putting their toys in order by the time you finish cleaning the dishes, and so on.

Establishing a game-like approach to get your strong-willed toddler to cooperate not only instills order in a fun way but also encourages your toddler to aim high. When you implement it right, this strategy activates the winner in your strong-willed toddler, and that winner will stop at nothing to get to the finishing line. It presents you with a priceless opportunity to raise a relentless toddler in a positive environment.

7

TAKING CARE OF THE PARENT

One of the major challenges of raising a strong-willed toddler is the ability to provide consistent attention and care despite their not-so-favorable attitude sometimes. Of course, you may face other problems such as financial challenges, inadequate sleep, and the inconveniences of having to reschedule your personal appointments when your parenting schedule clashes with that of your social life.

These issues can surely cause you to feel overworked, tired, and burnt out. So what do we do about all that, dear parent, dear caregiver? At one point or another, that time will come. It is your choice to prepare beforehand and take steps that can prevent your parental burnout or to just wait for the day your body gives up and you blackout. What is it going to be?

REFINING YOUR RELATIONSHIPS

Relationships that are loving, dependable, and responsive are absolutely necessary for the growth and well-being of your toddler. Your strong-willed toddler will feel more secure if you devote some of your precious time to establishing a close bond with them. They will have the confidence to go out and learn about the world when they have a sense of safety. Your strong-willed toddler will also learn how to think, interpret, communicate, conduct, display emotions, and develop social skills as they become more exposed to the world around them. During the toddler years, your little one experiences fast growth that will almost certainly result in shifts in the interaction between the two of you. If you are not careful enough, your strong-willed toddler might feel unloved or unwanted, causing them to withdraw from you and sometimes even the rest of the people around them.

Your strong-willed toddler will eventually realize that they are a unique person, and when they do, they will work hard to maintain and build onto that value. Your toddler desires to be self-sufficient in all aspects of their life, so if you deny them that, you deny them the essence of their life.

Once your strong-willed toddler makes up their mind about something, they may be reluctant about steering off their course to meet what you want. This sometimes makes parents and caregivers feel as though their toddler is disobedient and uncooperative, which can put a strain on the ties they have with their strong-willed toddlers. If you look at it from your little one's perspective and stay on the lookout for any red flags, you begin to understand why they sometimes set their decisions in stone.

Your strong-willed toddler may resist your efforts to put them in the care of others because they wouldn't want to be away from you. While that reflects well on your bond with them, it is proof of your toddler's poor social flexibility with those around them. Being with other people benefits your toddler's growth by significantly quickening the rate at which they can use and understand language. When they develop and improve their language skills, they gain the ability to participate in more group activities and games, as well as practice social skills such as taking turns and sharing. All these growth changes are important developmental goals that your strong-willed toddler might not acquire quickly if you are the only person they know. For that reason, it is important that you also help your strong-willed toddler create and refine connections with other individuals.

Your strong-willed toddler is still developing their emotions. They will experience a wide range of strong feelings, but they may not always be able to manage them or find the words to adequately convey them. It is possible that they might throw clothes, break toys, or scream in an effort to get their anger out. As you work toward refining your relationship with them, if you actively pay attention to their feelings, you may discover helpful ways to calm your strong-willed toddler. If you succeed in offering your toddler the support they need and provide them with love, care, and reassurance, then you succeed in strengthening the bonds you share with your strong-willed toddler.

During toddlerhood, your little one discovers that their actions can have an impact on the world around them. You may realize that your strong-willed toddler spends most of their time exploring new things and familiarizing themself with their environment. At this stage, they need you to stick around and encourage them to discover more things, so you may need to set aside more time with your strong-willed toddler than you did in the past.

Tips

Here are ways to improve your bonding time with your strong-willed toddler:

Stay Calm

Strong-willed toddlers tend to be difficult at times and are not immune to making blunders. However, as a parent or caregiver, you should remember that treating your strong-willed toddler with respect is equally as vital as disciplining your little one. You can still communicate well with your strong-willed little one, in a loving and calm manner even after they may have done something that necessitates you to reprimand them. Remember that yelling and physically punishing your strong-willed toddler is ineffective, so there really is no major point to go to such extents. Administering physical discipline or yelling also has the potential to negatively impact the quality of connection you have with your little one. Don't just wait to save your polite behavior for when you leave the house, but strive to ingrain it in your daily life. You can also teach your strong-willed toddler the basics of polite communication, such as thanking people when they receive something, excusing themself to deal with bathroom business and other gestures of politeness. Not only will you become closer to one another, but the atmosphere in your home will also become more pleasant if you treat each other with respect and decency.

Embrace Family Time

Having fun with your little one is one of the most effective methods to develop a closer relationship with them. Join them in going outside to play in a park and kicking a ball around. Or, you could grab a fun family board game and turn it into an educational game if you want to find something that intellectually challenges them and encourages them to work on great social skills and good manners while they are having fun. For example, they could learn how to behave graciously, whether they are the winner or the loser.

The fact that you are participating in something enjoyable together is much more essential than the action itself. You may watch movies geared toward youngsters, make or bake something, or read a storybook. Engage in an activity that brings you pleasure and allows you to connect with others at the same time, just as you would with your significant other.

Remember the Tight Embraces

Hugs and kisses are a wonderful way to bond with your strong-willed toddler and improve the bond you share. Spoil your little one with a lot of hugs whenever you can. This will show them just how much you love and appreciate them, and they will be more likely to give you hugs in return.

All Hands on Deck!

Strong-willed toddlers can provide a helping hand as long as they do not feel forced to do so. You can encourage this desire by assigning them reasonable duties and responsibilities that will help them feel more capable and loved. Do not hesitate to tell your little one how wonderful they are at their tasks and how much you value and appreciate their assistance. Not only will it bring you and your strong-willed toddler closer, but it will also help them further develop their positive qualities.

Show Your Love

Try to show your little one how much you care for them through simple gestures you can show on a daily basis. You can also throw in some fun by planning a vacation to places they seem to enjoy, spoiling them with their comfort foods, or even just having their friends over to play. Showing your strong-willed toddler some love doesn't have to cost rubies, but the love itself is more precious than gold. When you frequently show your strong-willed toddler how much they mean to you, you bolster the connection you share with them, making it stronger and more stable.

Connect With Family and Friends

It is crucial that you reconnect or strengthen the bonds you have with friends and family as you sail on this journey to raising your spirited toddler. This is important because it gives you an opportunity to learn new parenting techniques while resetting your mind from the hectic requirements of raising a strong-minded toddler. Another advantage of rekindling connections with friends and family is that they can help out with looking after your toddler in cases of emergencies or when you just need a break to take care of other affairs outside parenting.

Express Your Feelings

You will also benefit as a parent or caregiver from communicating your ideas and emotions with those who are close to you. Not only does that help build trust, but it also lets your loved ones know that you trust and cherish them just as much as they do you. Squeeze some time in your hectic parenting schedule to chat with your loved ones in order to prevent lapses in communication and to make space for helpful discussions. You can also use that connection time to listen to what your friends and family may be going through. That will prevent your relationships from being one-sided, thereby enhancing the relationships that you share with them. Simply devoting some of your time and focusing your attention on what they have to say is a vital step in the process of establishing a robust emotional connection.

Live Your Life

Do something with your life that interests you. It does not matter if they are just game nights, barbecues, or spontaneous adventures somewhere new. You need to make time for having fun in order to strengthen bonds with the people in your life, including friends and family. You can develop a stronger and more meaningful connection with the people who are closest to you by sharing the joys of everyday life with them and celebrating its simple pleasures. It helps to promote positivity in your relationships if you and your partner participate in enjoyable activities and have a good time together. Spending good times and celebrating with your loved ones and close friends helps to create memories that you can cherish for the rest of your life.

Practice Honesty

Several parents and caregivers end up miserable and depressed as a result of failing to manage emotions effectively. You may find yourself suppressing feelings, especially those of dissatisfaction, when someone wrongs you or fails to do their job properly. Imagine if you left your toddler in someone else's care and instructed them what to do and what not to, but you return to find that the person did everything wrong and their quality of work was very poor. Do you let them know that you are unhappy? Do you avoid leaving them with your little one next time? Or do you just ignore the mistake in order to avoid misunderstandings? Clear communication is essential to the maintenance of happy and successful relationships. It is necessary for you to communicate your perspectives and talk about the things that are important to you with those around you. That helps you achieve a greater level of mutual understanding while reducing the chances of stressing over unaddressed challenges that you bottled up inside you. You don't always have to talk about nice things; sometimes, it is okay to talk about the negative things that happen in life. If there are any concerns or disagreements between you and the people you interact with, you need to make an immediate effort to resolve the issues, even if it means having that difficult conversation.

Eat Together

Plan as many dinners as you can with your family, even if you won't be able to have everyone together all the time. Even if your weekday evenings are taken up by late shifts at work or extra activities, you can still find ways to spend time with your friends and family, such as by eating breakfast or snacks together. The most important thing is to keep in contact with your little one and make family mealtimes enjoyable for everyone by encouraging conversation about their days. Eating with your strong-willed toddler on a regular basis also increases their likelihood of achieving positive developmental outcomes, such as better health and eating habits, robust mental, emotional, and social skills, improved behavior, and better academic performance.

Take Responsibility

Several people find it difficult to accept when they are wrong. While you could have your reasons for not accepting your imperfections, it is very unwise to act right when you are wrong. That behavior not only makes it difficult for people to willingly deal with you in the future, but it also paints a negative approach to life in your strong-willed toddler's mind. Taking responsibility also applies to the way you carry out your parenting duties as a parent or caregiver. You cannot ask for help with everything as that may prevent you from bonding with your strong-willed toddler. Even if you have many reliable people helping you take care of your little one, some things really just require your special touch.

Share About Your Day

Having a conversation about what you did during the day is an excellent opportunity to catch up with your strong-willed little one on what they did. You can ask them questions that provoke detailed responses, such as what interesting things they did during the day. You can also tell your little one about your day, providing appropriate specifics to keep them interested. This will ensure that you get the most out of the conversation while deepening the bond you have with your little one and demonstrating to them how important they are to you.

PARENTING THERAPY

If all else fails, you have therapy, and it has your back too. Parenting therapy refers to a form of talk therapy that focuses on assisting parents and caregivers in navigating the challenges that come with nurturing strong-willed toddlers. Parenting therapy will assist you in recognizing, addressing, and managing your own experiences, both from the past and the present. If you have any unsettled business from the past which may be influencing the manner in which you interact with your spirited toddler, you can offload that burden during a parenting therapy session and walk out free again! In certain circumstances, parenting therapy can also assist you in improving communication with your partner or other people in the life of your free-spirited toddler. That will help you maintain a consistent and well-structured approach to parenting your strong-willed toddler.

Therapy gives you a priceless opportunity to discuss challenging aspects of parenting in an environment that is free from judgment, with the goal of improving your ability to handle the challenging aspects of raising a strong-willed toddler. In general, the goal of parenting therapy is to equip you with the information, resources, direction, and support you need to care for your spirited toddler in the healthiest and most effective manner possible.

You can start parenting therapy either by independently seeking help or after receiving recommendations from your primary health-care physician or psychologist. A counselor will then conduct an interview with you to discover your core challenges and concerns, develop a full grasp of the issue, and analyze your emotional state and behavior. Following the completion of the initial interview, the counselor will then be able to give you recommendations for therapy, if necessary.

You may require various therapeutic approaches in the event that one fails or falls short of your needs. Depending on the root of your problem, you may need services such as therapy for anger management, counseling for co-parenting, and many other programs. If, for example, you got hooked on alcohol while trying to cope with divorce, you may benefit from attending addiction therapy and therapy for dealing with divorce. In most cases, the first session of parenting therapy will only involve you and will center on the primary problem that you brought up during the initial interview.

Some of the benefits of attending parenting therapy include:

- valuable tips on how to respond to your spirited toddler
- strategies to solve family problems that may interfere with your parenting duties
- a safe space to offload and sort out your emotions without the fear or risk of being judged
- support during difficult parenting periods

Any parent or caregiver who admits they are having a hard time managing their parenting responsibilities may find parenting therapy very helpful. However, some parents or caregivers may benefit more from parenting therapy than others due to additional circumstances. Such instances may include:

- Parents and caregivers who are dealing with marital problems

Marriage problems such as financial struggles and infidelity can interfere with the positive upbringing you want for your toddler.

- Parents and caregivers who have a past history of abuse

Parents and caregivers who have suffered abuse may have challenges when raising their strong-willed toddlers.

- Parents and caregivers who have health issues

Health problems can be stressful and demanding at times, and raising a spirited toddler at the same time one is dealing with their health complications can decrease the total time and attention they can spend on their child.

- Parents and caregivers who are dealing with loss

Any major kind of loss can interfere with a parent or caregiver's ability to properly nurture their toddler. That could be the loss of a pet, a job, a loved one, or any other significant factor. The total result can cause a spirited child to act out, especially if it makes them feel abandoned.

• Parents and caregivers who are battling substance abuse

This one poses a variety of risks to the parent or caregiver as well as the strong-willed toddler involved. Substance abuse problems can trigger parenting mistakes such as neglect, inconsistency, violence, and so many more.

• Parents and caregivers who are processing divorce

This is a difficult change to adjust to, and that applies to both the parents and the strong-willed toddler involved. Divorce can steer the adults' focus to their own feelings, leaving strong-willed toddlers with limited attention.

Despite the numerous benefits of attending parental therapy, it is essential to keep in mind that there are also moments when it can be rather tough. To effectively process your feelings and move on with your life as a parent or caregiver, parenting therapy may require you to revisit some traumatic experiences from your past. Because of that, you could have feelings of anxiety or sadness while going through the therapy. However, it gets better, and it is worth it.

Some parents or caregivers experience frustration when parenting does not give them instant benefits. That can cause them to not take the process seriously, ignore the advice they get, or even quit. If you want to take on therapy while parenting, you need to commit and participate in the process for it to be successful. Most importantly, you need to be aware that this process is not instant and may cause you momentary discomfort in the beginning.

CONCLUSION

At this point, my hope is that you have understood and enjoyed this book. We dismissed some myths about strong-willed toddlers and discussed a few developmental phases during which your tiny human undergoes major growth changes. We also covered parental burnout and what you can do as a parent or caregiver to prevent the heat of parenting from burning you to char. Keep the fun going with the educational games that will help your spirited toddler stay interested while learning something for their growth.

If you found this book informative and helpful, please do share it with your family and friends so they may use some of the information to improve their parenting approaches.

REFERENCES

Brennan, D. (2021, June 15). *What to know about Erikson's 8 stages of development.* WebMD. https://www.webmd.com/children/what-to-know-eriksons-8-stages-development

CDC. (2020, October 6). *Infants & toddlers (approximate ages 0-3).* Centers for Disease Control and Prevention. https://www.cdc.gov/parents/infants/index.html

Cherry, K. (2006, February 13). *The sensorimotor stage of cognitive development.* Verywell Mind. https://www.verywellmind.com/sensorimotor-stage-of-cognitive-development-2795462

Cherry, K. (2022, January 21). *Single parenting stress: How to beat burnout.* Verywell Mind. https://www.verywellmind.com/single-parenting-stress-how-to-beat-burnout-5216180

Coor, N. (2021, September 19). *How to manage your anger and frustration as a parent.* Quick and Dirty Tips. https://www.quickanddirtytips.com/parenting/behavior/parent-anger-management

Duncan, A. (n.d.). *How you can relieve stress when you're a stay-at-home mom.* Verywell Family. https://www.verywellfamily.com/avoid-mommy-burnout-kids-all-day-4020217

Hattangadi, N., Cost, K. T., Birken, C. S., Borkhoff, C. M., Maguire, J. L., Szatmari, P., & Charach, A. (2020). Parenting stress during infancy is a risk factor for mental health problems in 3-year-old children. *BMC Public Health, 20*(1). https://doi.org/10.1186/s12889-020-09861-5

Hollman, L. (2016, June 24). *When parents feel helpless: Using 5 steps to parental intelligence.* HuffPost. https://www.huffpost.com/entry/when-parents-feel-helples_b_10635416

Mcleod, S. (2019, April 9). *Sensorimotor stage of cognitive development | simply psychology.* SimplyPsychology. https://www.simplypsychology.org/sensorimotor.html

Mcleod, S. (2022, April 6). *Jean Piaget's theory of cognitive development.* Simply Psychology. https://www.simplypsychology.org/piaget.html

Neece, C. L., Green, S. A., & Baker, B. L. (2012). Parenting stress and child behavior problems: A transactional relationship across time. *American Journal on Intellectual and Developmental Disabilities, 117*(1), 48–66. https://doi.org/10.1352/1944-7558-117.1.48

Pincus, D. (n.d.). *How to control your anger with kids.* Empowering Parents. https://www.empoweringparents.com/article/calm-parenting-get-control-child-making-angry/

Roskam, I., Raes, M.-E., & Mikolajczak, M. (2017). Exhausted parents: Development and preliminary validation of the parental burnout inventory. *Frontiers in Psychology, 8.* https://doi.org/10.3389/fpsyg.2017.00163

Sanvictores, T., & Mendez, M. D. (2021). *Types of parenting styles and effects on children.* PubMed; StatPearls Publishing. https://www.ncbi.nlm.nih.gov/books/NBK568743/

The Editors of Encyclopedia Britannica. (2018). Jean Piaget | Biography, Theory, & Facts. In *Encyclopædia Britannica.* https://www.britannica.com/biography/Jean-Piaget

Zapata, K. (2021, October 29). *Parental burnout: What it is and how to cope.* Healthline. https://www.healthline.com/health/parenting/parental-burnout

ABOUT THE AUTHOR

Sarah is a Mom to two young adults and a mad cockapoo called Bodie. As an early years practitioner and a single Mom raising strong willed children she's made it her mission to help others not make the same mistakes that she did and to help people see that it's a blessing to nurture and grow these tiny humans into strong, confident adults. When not found with a book in her hand or putting a pen to paper you'll find her on long walks in the great outdoors or fulfilling her other passion of filling pots full of colorful flowers in the garden.

Printed in Great Britain
by Amazon

33114108R00076